The Roots of Infidelity Go DEEEEP

Praise for Dewayne Williams' "Infidelity" Series!

"After reading this book, all I can do is stand in awe as I reflect on the mistakes I've made in my life. I found myself looking at the man in the mirror and asking, "What can I do to be a better man?" This book gets down to the deep-rooted issues most men deal with: self-esteem issues, parenting issues, growing up issues, and significant other issues. This made me reflect on my need to look within myself more deeply to gain a better understanding of my contributions to any given series of unfortunate circumstances that occur in my life. Take responsibility, be accountable, and start asking yourself, "What can I do to be better? What can I do to make things better?" This book is the purest mirror in that you will gain a better understanding of some of the things that have occurred in your relationships and how your contribution attributed to the outcome—past and present. If you didn't directly contribute, you tolerated it. Either way, you were the captain of your ship and had more control than you perhaps gave yourself credit. I believe this is a must-read book, with the ability to change the lives of its readers. It's one I will recommend to any family member or friend."

~ Joe Dupree Anderson, Radio Host

"After reading this book, it made me evaluate my past marriage. It helped by shedding light on how to live life to the fullest. This read made me want to reevaluate my time and approach to building new relationships. *The Roots of Infidelity Go DEEEEP* is the perfect guide!"

~ Bryson Bernard aka Cupid

"A coming of age story in a non-traditional narrative from the inner-workings of a single mom who has difficulty showing love to a young man who begins a destructive path of only wanting to be loved; this real and relevant retelling shows the dangers of a broken soul on the path to find wholeness with a bit of humor intermingled. Whether you have been the unfaithful or you have been on the receiving end, you will question yourself, the role your upbringing truly played on who you have become, and be challenged to end the vicious cycle and reclaim your life through truth."

~ Dana Senegal

The Roots of Infidelity Go DEEEEP

"Dewayne Williams is a master of writing and applying appropriate words as well as actions to keep your attention! He also shares and explores situations involving illicit relationships within the church setting, which is often a taboo subject. I was hooked on reading just from the FLASHBACK CHAPTER! There are superb scriptural references throughout and is recommended for both men and women. One of the many quotes I loved was "Tell the Truth and Shame the Devil." EXCELLENT, EXCELLENT - yet another award winner by Pearly Gates Publishing, LLC!"

~ Creative NANA

"This book touched on a lot of areas that will have you looking at situations in a whole new light. To my good friend, Dewayne Williams: Excellent job on the book!"

~ Clementine Parker

"[Applause] Clearly articulated and defined to a point of fear from my own past experiences in life. This book has opened my eyes to a new level of understanding infidelity and broken relationships because of it. I found myself reading a portion of the book, pausing to think, and then consequently reliving the actions and reactions of my past over and over again in my mind. This passage will not only help me going forward, but will guide me somewhat as how to model myself better as a husband, father of young men, and as a leader in my family. I have been Joseph...honestly damn near every male I call a friend has been Joseph or a mere portion of him at some point in their lives! Bravo DeWayne Williams, Bravo!"

~ Juan Alexander

"This book is a MUST READ!! A great story!! A book that everyone can relate to!! Looking forward to another book from this phenomenal author!!"

~ Lizza Sam

The Roots of Infidelity Go DEEEEP

"This was a very good read that relates to all relationships, races, and especially religions. There are so many people in churches who are unfaithful and choose not to discuss it and "play" church. I am from Opelousas, Louisiana and come across both broken men and women who are playing games to deceive the other person. These acts not only hurt both individuals in the end but like the author mentioned, children suffer the most. In conclusion, individuals should seek a relationship with God instead of religion from these lost churches filled with lost men and women. Great read and kudos to the author for being real enough to mention this topic."

~ Dametra Taylor

Dewayne Williams

The Roots of Infidelity Go DEEEEP

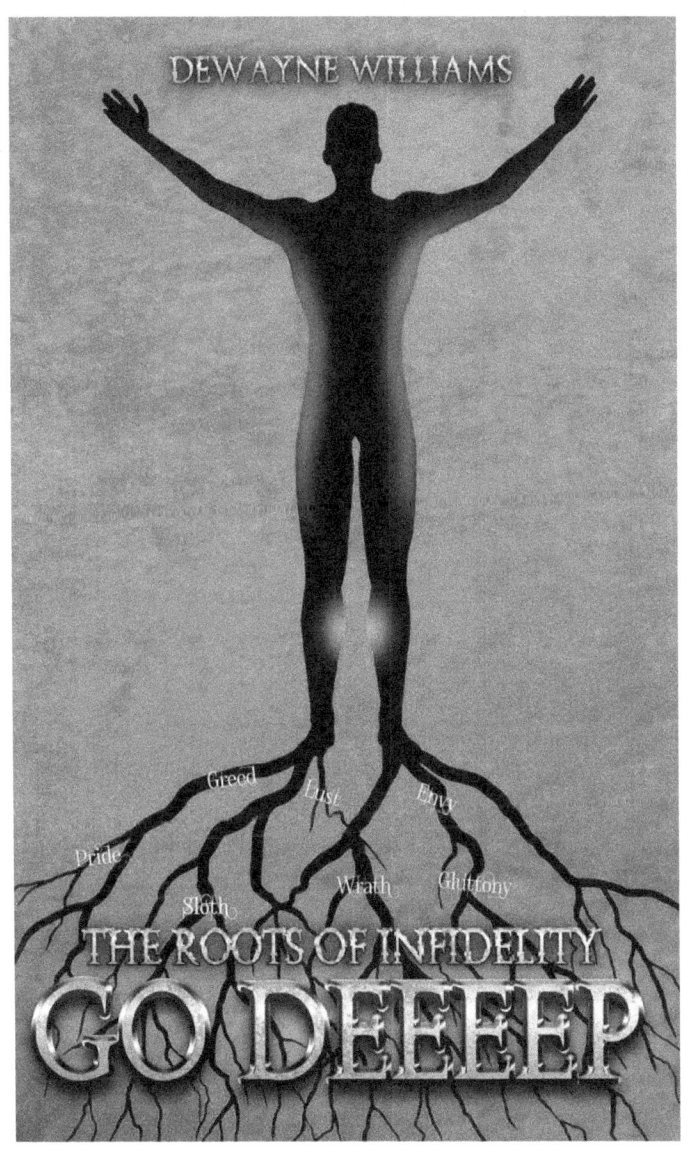

Dewayne Williams

THE ROOTS OF INFIDELITY
GO DEEEEP

International Best-Selling Author

Dewayne Williams

Pearly Gates Publishing, LLC, Houston, Texas

The Roots of Infidelity Go DEEEEP

The Roots of Infidelity Go DEEEEP

Copyright © 2018
Dewayne Williams

All Rights Reserved. Printed in the United States of America. No portion of this publication may be reproduced, stored in an electronic system, or transmitted in any form or by any means (electronic, mechanical, photocopy, recording, or otherwise) without written permission from the author or publisher. Brief quotations may be used in literary reviews.

ISBN 13: 978-1-945117-77-0
Library of Congress Control Number: 2018933851

Unless otherwise indicated, scripture references are taken from the New International Version (NIV) of the Holy Bible and used with permission by Zondervan.
Public Domain.

This book is a work of fiction. Names, characters, businesses, places, events, locales, and incidents are either the products of the author's imagination or used in a fictitious manner. Any resemblance to actual persons, living or dead, or actual events is purely coincidental.

For information and bulk ordering, contact:
Pearly Gates Publishing, LLC
Angela R. Edwards, CEO
P.O. Box 62287
Houston, TX 77205
BestSeller@PearlyGatesPublishing.com

DEDICATION

This book is dedicated to everyone who is still dealing with unhealed wounds. I know that life can be difficult just by trying to live in today's world. I also know that when we add to life's challenges by not dealing with our demons, we contribute to keeping the world in a bad place.

Additionally, I would like to dedicate this book to every person who has lashed out at others as a result of not dealing with their open wounds. The easiest thing for us to do is say we were either born this way or forced to be this way as a result of things that took place in our past. We never consider how that mindset maintains our stagnancy. We get older but never truly grow! We look back but never see from where we came. We find ourselves reliving the same things over and over because we don't acknowledge that we are a part of the problem. Once we get to that point, then and only then will we see that we can become better as individuals.

So, to everyone in this world, I say: Live with a mindset of being true to yourself!

The Roots of Infidelity Go DEEEEP

PREFACE

Trying to live life to the fullest can be a daunting task when you consider the people in your life that your choices will affect. Knowing the direction in which to go will prove its worth if you choose a path that allows you that opportunity. To know and still choose a different path can make one seem a bit insane, to say the least.

For me, that was my story. I could see the dead end up ahead, yet I chose to embark on that journey because, at that time in my life, I was prepared to ride that train until the wheels fell off. I was on the hunt for (at minimum) a moment of temporary happiness. If I could only tough out what I thought was happiness for that moment, I would be satisfied—or so I thought. Craziness is a complete understatement. The truth is what I thought was happiness was nothing more than mere moments of selfishness…without a happy ending.

The only reason I wrote this particular book is simple: To help save one relationship at a time! Having seen the pain on so many people's faces after dealing with issues of infidelity, it was clear to me that I could use my pain and horrid experiences to help others who are going through issues. While everyone has their reasons for doing what they do, I am of the belief that the root causes are buried inside of old wounds that have not been healed. To make matters worse, our actions affect the children we bring into this world.

Cheating can be viewed as a disease. So many people are infected with "it" and, often, cannot see what awaits them in the future. Of course, I am not God—neither do I claim to want to be Him; however, if God can use me as a mouthpiece or vessel to help steer people off the path of destruction, I am all in for Him!

I have been the victim of sexual abuse and suffered from insecurities. My past includes a host of many other painful issues that you will read about soon. As well, I have been the cheater and hurt others. I have seen both sides of the coin and know for certain: This, too, shall pass.

When we can live in truth, we know that we will be aligned with the realities of life. My goal is not to relatively live truth. It is to live truth in an absolute state! By living this way, we can ALL be free from those things that purposely hinder us from growing.

INTRODUCTION

<u>Infidelity.</u> An action that affects more than what is on the surface.

<u>Infidelity.</u> It resides in the very depths of one's mind **and** soul — more than any other secret thought tossed into the seas of forgiving and forgetting. One may *say* they forgive, yet find themselves remaining shackle-bound to forgetting.

Let me introduce to some and reintroduce to others, Joseph. Like other men in this blood-sucking world, Joseph has faced many challenges all throughout his life. Although many are self-inflicted, others are products of what people in today's society view as "the new normal". To that, I say "Bull Crap!"

On the pages of this book, you will be introduced to a host of characters that you will connect with — in one way or another. Will you 'see' yourself, your significant other, family members, or friends? Chances are likely you will identify with each in some capacity. That is where your ugly truth will be exposed once and for all.

The Roots of Infidelity Go DEEEEP

I intend to speak to **THAT** person…the one who's been in turmoil behind secrets that destroy from the inside out. I do not doubt that what you have been hiding in the darkness is affecting your relationships (not just romantic) on various levels. Chances are you don't even make the connection, and if you **DO**, you are either living a guilt-ridden life or could care less about the person whom you're offending.

Enter in *The Roots of Infidelity Go DEEEEP*.

Throughout any relationship with challenges, we may find ourselves believing the adage that states, *"The grass is **DEFINITELY** greener on the other side."* Before we know it, we begin exploring the thoughts of the 'other side' of the relationship. Thoughts lead to actions. Those senses that we once turned off — for whatever the reason — are now ablaze in all of their glory! Three things then happen (and no matter how hard you **try** to control them, it's futile):

1. The slightest thing your mate does annoys you at every turn; and

2. The slight of another's scent intrigues you; or even worse,
3. You entertain the idea of your life being better with 'that other person'.

Interestingly enough, you know you have crossed into forbidden territory without so much as meandering across the street after "it". Your mind begins to take control, and before you know it, someone else is occupying your "first thing in the morning thoughts". That, my friend, is how the roller coaster keeps its momentum. Have you ever considered why a roller coaster is designed with a bunch of twists and turns? The answer is simple — and relatable: The design is purposed to build up and maintain the thrill of the ride from start to finish. Once the ride is over, you are then faced with a decision (*choices, choices, choices…*):

- Find that you have been fulfilled and never ride again; OR

- Ride it over and over again, seeking more satisfaction with each new undertaking.

The Roots of Infidelity Go DEEEEP

Should you opt for the latter, you've missed the point: It's just a ride. The feeling is only ***temporary***.

Too often, we miss life's lessons. They are **right there**, but the plainness of their view is overlooked. We become so focused on what we *think* the outcome will be that the actual objective is undermined. But hey, how can you blame a person, right? The mind, body, and soul want what they want…when they want it!

Let's pause for just a moment to think it through.

The truth is this: The rush we get while living in the moment is unexplainable. The **heart** beats faster at the mere thought of the other side. The **hands** become clammy at the mere thought of the other side. Butterflies flutter in the pits of the **belly** at the mere thought of the other side. Those thoughts dig ***DEEEEP***, making our fantasy-turned-reality more relevant than other things we've ever experienced in life.

All too well, we can easily recall the moment "it" all began…

Dewayne Williams

TABLE OF CONTENTS

PRAISE FOR DEWAYNE WILLIAMS' "INFIDELITY SERIES!	III
DEDICATION	XII
PREFACE	XIII
INTRODUCTION	XVI
JOSEPH'S REFLECTIONS	1
TO TOSS OR NOT TO TOSS	7
WHO HOLDS THE CARDS?	15
EYE CANDY GALORE!	21
THE FOREST FOR THE TREES	29
THE OTHER SIDE OF THE HAND	37
TOUCHING THE SURFACE	51
JOSEPH'S HAUNTING MEMORIES	57
SORRY…NOT SORRY	65
SOOTHING THERAPY	73
SURPRISE, SURPRISE, SURPRISE!	95
THOUGHTS, THE OPEN ROAD, AND A GUN	99
FUNCTIONING IN BROKENNESS	105
HE MADE ME TOUCH HIM	117
CAUGHT UP IN WHAT IT ISN'T	123
THE TEMPTRESS HAS ARRIVED!	129
LEAVE THAT TITLE AT THE DOOR	137

GOOD INTENTIONS AND DEMONS	147
THERE'S ALWAYS A HEFTY PRICE TO PAY	153
WHEN YOU'VE DONE ALL TO STAND	161
LOYAL TO 'SELF' ONLY	163
LET YOUR LIFE SPEAK YOUR WORTH	173
THE BODY SPEAKS	181
TEMPTATIONS AND PLEAS	185
HELP IS ONE THOUGHT AWAY	193
FRACTURED; NOT QUITE BROKEN	195
THE SICK MERRY-GO-ROUND	199
HE VIOLATED ME—I'M A BOY!	207
THE WARNING SIGNS WERE THERE!	211
WHAT ABOUT ME?	221
WAIT A MINUTE! YOU'RE WHAT?	227
THE "SHIFT"	237
LOYALTY? WHAT'S THAT?	241
SECRETS EXPOSED	245
A LITTLE BIT OF THIS…A LOT OF THAT	251
CONCLUSION	259
ABOUT THE AUTHOR	277
CONTACT THE AUTHOR	279
LETTER TO MY FUTURE WIFE	281
FEEL FREE TO QUOTE ME!	283

The Roots of Infidelity Go DEEEEP

JOSEPH'S REFLECTIONS

So many nights of reflection and turmoil at the same time…

It's 3:33 a.m. I'm sitting here bright-eyed and bushy-tailed, somewhat spaced out! I'm so overwhelmed; I literally cannot think clearly. My muddled thoughts are overpowering all of my other senses. I was awakened from my slumber by an onslaught of nightmares that starred **ME**…all alone in the world.

What does a person do when the weight of the world appears to be on their shoulders? You can't focus on one problem too long because others are waiting their turn in line. The overwhelming feeling can leave you believing you're neglecting the other problems as if they are your children, abandoned without a care in the world for them.

The more I try to prepare my mind to pray and quiet my spirit-man, the more difficult it appears to be. If given the opportunity to illustrate what I think is happening to me, I would compare it to a volcano erupting and taking over a small town…slowly, but surely. The lava is **hot**! The heat from the belly of the earth is being felt from miles away. As it nears, I am aware of its all-consuming nature, reaching out with its embers to burn me from the soles of my feet to the tip of my head in an instant—or so it *appears*. I'm trying vehemently to scream for **HELP**, but no sound makes it past my lips.

While nailed to the cross on Calvary, Jesus Christ uttered the words, *"My God, My God: Why hast Thou forsaken Me?"* Forget the concern about the infection that was sure to set in from the rusty nails being bashed into His body or how His ligaments were ripped apart as His earthly flesh dangled from that cross. Jesus' simple cry was (in plain speak), *"God, why have You allowed me to go through so much pain? Can't You just take away this pain faster than the blink of an eye? No. You wanted me to go through this. I had to go through this. For what? For whom?"*

That raises some questions for me: Did Jesus understand His purpose **before or after** His last breath on earth? Did God answer Him on the cross **or** when He ascended to Heaven? Some might say we will never know that answer until we make it to Heaven. If that is true, how does anyone expect me to figure out my issues in the here and now?

The sad reality for many is this: People give their all to another person, only to find out they have been made a fool of for months…sometimes, even *years*. They find themselves sitting up waiting for their significant other to come home, all the while knowing that person is away from the home because he/she is loving on someone else. How could that be defined as "living"?

Where is the strength that God says I have? God is an All-Knowing God, so He had to know this day would come. I can't help but wonder why. Was it to save me? Was it for me to use my pain to help others? Who knows for sure? All I know is that at this point in my life, I wouldn't wish this suffering on anyone.

In a moment of transparency, I can honestly see why some people decide to say, "Screw it!", and pull the trigger.

Disclaimer: While I dibbled and dabbled with that thought a few times in my life, I want to make it *clear* that I'm saying I am empathetic. **I do not encourage nor endorse that course of action.**

I feel I have been on the run for far too long...from myself. Every time something gets tough, I look for an 'out'. I know I'm not the only one.

You! Yes, you — the one reading this very sentence — have also tried to run away from your problems before, huh? Why? Are you afraid to admit you've been played by another as well? Forget about living in the past, my friend. I am talking about **RIGHT NOW**...at this very moment.

It's time for me to "man up" and convince myself not to run this time. It's time for me to stand firm in the quicksand and take whatever comes. The challenge is that I feel like I've *BEEN* taking it. I know, I know; it's contradictory. One minute, I'm standing; the next, I'm running. I suppose this is one of my 'standing' moments. Who knows? My thoughts are all over the place. I'll be honest here: I'm scared — of myself. I'm looking over my shoulders. I hear sounds at night and voices in my head that tell me she's cheating. If she is (which I'm sure of), she can simply say she wants out of the relationship, correct?

People like 'her' (cheaters) will have you questioning yourself. *Who am I? What am I?* At times, I feel I can be Satan's right-hand man by stepping outside of the relationship as well. Tit-for-tat, yes? Other times, I feel I should be God's mouthpiece by remaining faithful. <u>Choices, choices, choices.</u> I **feel** I can be both simultaneously, but the problem remains: Which do I want? If everlasting life is my choice, then what has me shackled to 'self'? If everlasting life is **not** my choice, then why am I so afraid of intentionally hurting her? I can remember a time not so long ago when I did "bad" things, and it appeared I didn't have a care in the world about doing them; who I hurt didn't matter. The reality is that those experiences haunt me quite often. The things I've seen, done, heard, and helped are beyond crazy. Still, I feel the guilt from it **ALL**.

There is a saying that when people lie so much, they tend to believe their own lies. If I had a dollar for every time I lied, Bill Gates would be calling me for loans. I decided to tell the truth only when it mattered to or benefited me. To be honest, that is quite sad. I suppose because I have a history of telling untruths, even my truths were deemed lies. *Damned if I do…damned if I don't.* What in the world did anyone do to me to deserve my barrage of lies?

So, this brings me back to our All-Knowing God; The One that says, *"Repent and turn away from your wicked ways."* Does it **really** take all of this torment to prove a point, Lord? Must I continue to live in this world and deny all that it has to offer?

It all seems very sick to me at times…

The Roots of Infidelity Go DEEEEP

TO TOSS OR NOT TO TOSS

It's time to face the hard truth: Is **now** the time to throw in the towel? I'm not necessarily referring to ending the relationship, but rather throwing in the towel on neglecting your feelings. You—and only you—know how you feel when you lay down at night. Do you experience that gut-wrenching feeling when you know something is "off", yet you are too afraid to deal with the idea of confronting those feelings head-on? How many more times will you allow your intelligence to be played on? You were built to withstand things as it relates to your survival. **Infidelity shouldn't be one of them.** Sure, you can make it through with work (if both of you want that). I am not talking about the theory of simply pouring out your hearts with an expected outcome. Here: Let me make it plain:

STOP PLAYING THE FOOL!

I'm sure you've heard it before, but I'm going to say it again: *People will do what you allow them to do*. Of course, any one of the seven deadly sins—**Pride, Greed, Lust, Envy, Sloth, Wrath, or Gluttony**—can be a reason for someone to cheat, but much of what they do is because they know they can get away with it, if only for a moment in time. As for me, I am at a point where I hate seeing people hurting.

Here's some more hard truth: *You can't always trust the people you call 'friends.'* Sadly enough, someone in your circle has either had thoughts about being with your significant other, had a conversation you know nothing about with him or her, or (even worse) have had sexual relations with the person you call "mate".

Another disclaimer: PLEASE don't get it twisted. This is **NOT** a call-to-action to be friendless. Rather, I am alerting you to the foolery that can take place right under your nose.

Think about it, though: Do you think you are the *ONLY* person who finds your mate attractive **or** are you absent-minded enough to think everyone **outside** of your circle can find that person attractive, but not those you call friends? **STOP. IT. RIGHT. NOW.** People have eyes and body parts that naturally react to what they see. Many make an intentional effort to resist the pervasive thoughts, but 'mistakes happen'. That brings about the question: Are they friends or

The Roots of Infidelity Go DEEEEP

not? Should infidelity rear its ugly head, you would likely place more blame on the friend rather than the person with whom you lay. Why is that? Oh! *Loyalty, you say?* Hell, loyalty is easy to toss into the air when it suits you. Let a nice proposition come your way… Yeah, yeah. I know. You strongly disagree, right? Well, let's use the following analogy:

Do you ever wonder why people change their shoes when their feet hurt? The most **obvious** reason is because the shoes don't fit the feet properly; hence, the discomfort. **BUT** you fell in love with either the look of the shoes or the image the shoes give you. You will continue to wear the shoes that cause you pain because you desire the attention they indirectly give you. *HOWEVER*, the shoes have no sense of loyalty to you because they serve one purpose: to provide cover for your feet. That's it! Nothing more, nothing less. Now, let your feet hurt bad enough in those shoes, and you **will** remove them. Those shoes are no different than the person you *KNOW* you shouldn't be with, but you continue to expect loyalty—when that person isn't capable of being loyal…at least not to **YOU**! There is a set of feet out there looking for the perfect-fitting shoes, just like there is a person out there who will be loyal to you (and vice-versa).

There are many driving forces that prompt people to do the things they do. Often, the signs are hidden very well. I want you to stop right now and ask yourself this question:

Am I paying attention to the signs or am I settling and holding on tightly to the towel?

Please don't misunderstand my message here. You see, I truly believe love is a beautiful thing. True love affords you someone to call your own. True love provides you with someone you can have the most fun. True love gives you a shoulder on which to cry. True love brings you someone who will think of you when you don't even think of yourself. Often, we *don't* consider those things to be signs of "true love". Yes, the person loves you; however, times may have changed, and they are at a place where the things that used to excite them in the past simply don't do it for them any longer. As for you, you may find yourself having thoughts of how to make things better before both of you become bitter. You have those thoughts, but no action.

The Roots of Infidelity Go DEEEEP

You go about your day operating in the same routine, hoping and praying that by some miracle, God would come down, tap you on the shoulder, and give you and your mate just what you need.

The reality is that you've had "it" all along! What is that "it"? **The desire to fix "it"!**

If this is your situation, it's time to be honest with yourself. You know that *DEEEEP* down inside, there is an identifiable problem. You live with and through it daily. What you don't have are the answers to the many questions mentally-imposed on yourself. My, my, my...the mind is a terrible thing to waste—if you don't deal with it!

Communication is the key.

The difficult conversations are truly the ones that will make most relationships stronger. As a people, we have been conditioned to think that sharing our true thoughts will only make things worse because the person on the receiving end won't be able to handle the **raw** truth. What if we looked at it from a different vantage point?

We go about life thinking he/she feels one type of way. Years pass, and you are taken aback after learning all that you thought you knew was a blatant lie. I am confident it would **NOT** sit well with you. In fact, I would go so far as to suggest that you would probably look at that person differently—so much so that it could cost you your relationship. Now, stop and consider this: Have you ever considered the many times he/she tried to talk to you and you reverted to your way of thinking, came across as downright rude, and remained unwilling to simply listen? To make the situation worse, you were so wrapped up in your thoughts, you still didn't see that *you* were the problem! Of course, you didn't **THINK** you were the problem, as your significant other chose to not make an issue out of "it". However, experience has proven that you are so wrapped up in yourself, that when any issue—whether big or small— is presented, you respond the same way every single time: like a volcano erupting. How can *anything* be accomplished if you are a walking time bomb ready to explode at any given moment?

The Roots of Infidelity Go DEEEEP

There are so many dynamics and facets to a relationship. To consume each could be likened to trying to eat an entire, full-grown elephant in one sitting—tusks included. Time passes and tensions rise. Before you know it, both of you are questioning the validity of the relationship. Thoughts *(here they come crossing the street)* start to roam and, before you know it, you find yourself fighting the **person** rather than fighting the elephant in the room: **SELFISHNESS IN ITS PUREST FORM!** More time passes, and you start to go through the *motions* of being in a 'relationship'. That in itself *NEVER* has the best of outcomes.

The point here is simply this: Know where the **ROOT** of the issues began before you throw in the towel. Dig *DEEEEP*!

"Flee also youthful lusts; but pursue righteousness, faith, love [and] peace…"

2 Timothy 2:22

The Roots of Infidelity Go DEEEEP

WHO HOLDS THE CARDS?

The phone vibrates. It's Chasity— 'that friend' you have known for some time now. As usual, she is trying to link up with you, as tonight is "the night". Both of you are in need of that long, overdue drink. The plans are set. *"I will be ready around 11"*, is your reply to her.

You grab yourself a pregame drink while listening to Pandora play in the background. Sipping and slowly getting yourself into the mood, you walk over to the closet and stand there for a minute. You look over your selection of gear, trying to decide what to wear. You anticipate on it being a **GOOD** night. "Bar 30" is the new spot in the city. Any and everyone is typically there, and the chances of running into an old friend is always a possibility.

~~~~~~~~~~

The phone rings on Brandy's nightstand. It's Patrick (Pat) calling. She refuses to allow him to mess up her mood. After all, the two of them haven't been on the same page for quite some time now. Knowing Pat, he will keep calling until she answers, but what the hell? She's screwed either way. If she **doesn't** answer, it will be an issue because his insecurities will have him automatically assuming she's with some other man. If she **does** answer, there's still no win because he has underlying issues that have nothing to do with her. She could do without the arguing today.

~~~~~~~~~~

For context, Pat has been dating Brandy for a while. Pat knew that Brandy wasn't all the way '100' in the beginning of their relationship, but he was truly trying to be 'that guy'. He wanted to make Brandy happy for the rest of her life. As for Brandy, she knew Pat's heart was in the right place, but because of the past hurts she endured, her insecurities would not allow her to put anything past anyone. Her trust-factor was *LOW*.

Then there's David. He was in the picture long before Pat. The problem with David was that he wasn't ready for a commitment when they first met. Brandy wanted something serious, but David had a lifestyle that suited him just fine without the constant companionship of a steady relationship. He was a promoter and heavy into the club scene. He was well-known and knew all of the hot spots to go on any given day. From the onset, Brandy knew that wasn't the type of lifestyle she wanted to live; wondering and worrying all the time about what he was doing and with whom.

Brandy purposefully distanced herself from David, yet she was still comfortable with him when they did spend time together. What was unfortunate about that level of comfort was that he knew what buttons to push and when to push them. To Brandy's defense, she still held all the cards…in a way. She knew David was trying hard to get into her world and build a relationship, and that played into her favor. She found herself being able to control the atmosphere when they saw each other.

~~~~~~~~~~

Pat was truly in touch with his life. He knew Brandy wasn't all the way in and strongly-suspected there **had** to be someone else connected to her. There were times when he could reach her all times of the day and night; other times, she was ghost. What had her attention so much that she would outright *ignore* his repeated calls?

You might wonder, ***"Why keep calling her, then?"*** Well, for Pat, the experiences he had in life weren't all positive when calls went unanswered, and he hoped for a different end as it related to Brandy.

The most recent incident was when he tried calling a now-former girlfriend and having his calls ignored. Later, he caught her leaving a hotel with another man. When he continued to press the issue about her repeated absences and lack of respect, he learned that even her weekly grocery store runs involved deception: She was, indeed, seeing someone else. So, you see, for Pat, having his calls ignored never ended well. In his mind, he felt that if he kept calling, she would eventually pick up the phone and all would be well in his world.

~~~~~~~~~~

It was no surprise when Brandy didn't pick up at times. He was unsure if she was trying to set a tone of making it known that she will answer when she gets good and ready or if she had more respect for another man than for him.

~~~~~~~~~~

The Roots of Infidelity Go DEEEEP

Brandy's phone rang again. She noticed it was Pat's third time calling, so she picked up. *"Hello?"* she began. Immediately, Pat let her know he was bothered by taking a jab. *"I guess you sleep better at night seeing me calling and not answering the phone."*

That was just the "out" she needed for the night. The argument ensued…

"You're not my damn daddy! I answer* MY *phone when I please!"

She was banking on Pat taking the bait…and he did. After a few minutes of yelling back and forth, Brandy hung up the phone on him. That, of course, drove Pat crazy. The gut feeling he'd had all day was starting to play itself out. He wanted to spend time with Brandy to try to work through their issues, but she was having no parts of it.

On this night, Brandy's emotions were all over the place. Mad. Happy. Ready to party and have fun. And also knowing she needed to decide with whom she wanted to be. Day by day, her choices were growing slimmer. She knew she needed to make a choice, but one more night wouldn't change that...or would it?

The Roots of Infidelity Go DEEEEP

EYE CANDY GALORE!

After their argument, Pat finally received a text from Brandy stating that she was going out with Chasity. He knew what *that* meant. Chasity was single and 'out there' with hers. **Anything** was bound to happen when in her company.

Pat's wrath started taking over his mind. Wrestling back and forth with his thoughts, he called his homeboy, Joseph.

~~~~~~~~~~

For those of you who don't already know, Joseph is a man who has been through hell and back—*especially* when it came to women. His world was turned upside down as a young boy when he was molested. After dealing with that ugly secret for many years, he didn't realize how not addressing it ignited the fire within him to go buck wild…and buck **WILD** he went.

Joseph and Pat met at work years ago. Joseph knew bits and pieces about the situation between Pat and Brandy.

"What up?" Joseph asked as he answered the phone. *"I'm thinking of hitting the streets tonight,"* responded Pat. *"Where to?"* Joseph suggested the hottest spot in the city—the same place Brandy **might** be. Immediately, Pat rejected that idea, as he had no desire to possibly be in the same club as Brandy. He sure as hell didn't want her thinking he was following her. After some dialogue, the two settled on visiting a hookah bar that was low-key and popping at the same time.

As usual, Joseph knew half the crowd there. Pat tried his best to enjoy himself, but his mind was racing with thoughts of Brandy. They got settled at a table in the middle of the room, ordered their drinks, and indulged in the hookah at their table. Pat's vibe soon began to mellow out. The music was on point, and there was a lot of eye candy in the building.

As Pat glanced over at the door, in walked David. Although Pat knew David from around the way, he didn't know that **HE** was the man who had captured Brandy's attention. David walked over to their table and gave Pat the standard 'dap'—the way brothers in the hood acknowledged respect for one another. They conversed for a moment, and David stated he was club-hopping that evening, with nothing major planned. The conversation was short and sweet, as the eye candy was everywhere…calling all of their names.

As the night progressed, Pat and Joseph had drinks sent over to their table. The waitress whispered, *"From the table over there,"* as she pointed to a table where three beautiful ladies were seated. Of course, one of the men had to say 'Thank you,' right? Of course! Joseph walked over and stood speaking to the ladies for about five minutes. To Pat, it seemed like an eternity. After the excruciating wait, the new 'party of four' headed to where Pat sat anxiously waiting.

"Thank you for the drink!" Pat addressed all three ladies. Not knowing the specifics of who made the purchase, he felt it was the right thing to do by acknowledging the gesture with sincere gratitude. Introducing himself, he shook the hand of each of the ladies.

Taking a more observant look, he locked eyes with one who stirred up his 'man bone'. He was faced with a decision: Indulge in the moment or stay true to his commitment to Brandy *(although in his heart, he knew she wasn't the least bit concerned about him…at least not right now)*. Pat opted for the latter choice.

"While I appreciate the drink and conversation, I do have someone at home." That reply was in response to the question presented about whether or not he had a girlfriend. With a flirtatious confidence, all three ladies agreed that they have the utmost respect for a man who is true to his lady.

Joseph, on the other hand, let it be known that he was single and free to mingle. He even went so far as to openly suggest that Pat's commitment was that of a *"real man and that Pat was a better man than him"*. Well, that comment opened the door for the barrage of questions that followed.

Why was Pat a better man?

Do you [Joseph] not believe in monogamous relationships?

What are you [Joseph] looking for in a mate?

The Roots of Infidelity Go DEEEEP

How long have you [Joseph] been single?

What was going on in your [Pat's] relationship that caused Joseph to take a jab?

Wow! These women were inquisitive and sharp!

Well, since they asked, Pat chose to reluctantly share bits and pieces of his relationship issues with these "strangers". Of course, each had her own opinion on what he should do, but there was one constant piece of advice: Move on because Brandy clearly wasn't ready. That advice didn't make the night any better for him. Still…perhaps they were right.

Trying her best to keep the conversation light and friendly, Jules (the one Pat found **beyond** gorgeous) said, *"Look, I respect what you have going on. However, I can't help but think how great of a man you seem to be. No, I don't know you, but I feel I am good at reading people. You, my friend, are solid. Given that, I won't ask for your number, but here's mine"*. She wrote her number down on a napkin and extended it to him, just out of his reach. Pat hesitated, and she could sense his unease. Jules continued, *"If you don't feel* *comfortable putting my number in your phone, hit me up on Instagram at Jules_the_Solid_One."*

Faced with yet another awkward decision, Pat pulled out his phone, logged in to Instagram, and clicked to 'Follow' her.

"I think it is best I not take your number, but hey; you seem like good people. Instagram it is!"

Looking for an opportunity to step away to give some air to the situation, Pat excused himself from the table and headed to the men's room. On the way, he sent Brandy a *"WYD?"* (What you doing?) text. *"Nothing."* She replied **instantly**! *"Where are you?"*, Pat asked. *"Club-hopping,"* came the **instant** response. Of course, Pat wanted specifics. As was typical, Brandy chose to leave that part out. *"WYA?"* (Where you at?), she texted. Before he replied, his insecurity took over. He wrestled with why she asked when she wouldn't even tell him precisely where ***SHE*** was.

All sorts of questions popped up in his head: *Does she want to see me? Is she trying to figure out where I am so that she doesn't go 'there'? Is she trying to make other plans with someone else and needs to know how long I'll be occupied?*

The Roots of Infidelity Go DEEEEP

After a short delay, he replied, *"Doing the same with Joseph." "Oh."* Confused by the context of the shortness of her reply, he texted, *"Missing you and hoping to see you soon." "K"*, she replied.

At that moment, he knew their situation still had not smoothed over with her. Some time apart and not communicating would ease the tension. Typically, they wouldn't let no more than four hours go by without saying *something* to each other, especially on the weekend. If time didn't heal this wound, some drinks definitely would!

Pat's mind went wandering…

"Therefore, whether you eat or drink, or whatever you do, do all to the glory of God."

1 Corinthians 10:31

The Roots of Infidelity Go DEEEEP

THE FOREST FOR THE TREES

After exiting the restroom, Pat stopped at the bar to grab a round of drinks for the table. When he arrived with drinks in hand, Jules mentioned that she was patiently awaiting his return. Oh boy. The attraction was mutual. Temptation was sitting across from him in all its splendor. Meanwhile, fear of his reality—that Brandy was with someone else—wreaked havoc in his head.

Conversation between Jules and Pat continued to grow deeper. Innocent flirting began. Subtle love taps and flirtatious words flowed freely back and forth. Before they knew it, it was 2:00 a.m.! The club lights illuminated the space and Joseph said, *"The party continues! On to the next destination!"*

Pat, holding firm to his commitment to Brandy, said that he was calling it a night. Although he enjoyed Jules' company, he was distracted. He felt a strong need to reach Brandy and spend quality time with her. He knew Joseph was going to be just fine with his newly-acquired friends who had agreed to head to the strip club for more fun. Joseph tried (and failed) to have Pat tag along. Even when Joseph pulled him to the side and suggested he see the forest for the trees, Pat knew he would make everyone's night dull with his company. The life Joseph was suggesting he live was not his style anymore. The look of disappointment was evident on Jules' face, but deep down inside, her level of respect for him grew leaps and bounds in that moment.

Once in his car and on his way home, he called Brandy. Before hitting 'Call', he felt something was off. He didn't expect an answer, and the voicemail on the other end didn't disappoint. His heart started to race as his blood pressure began to rise. He couldn't understand why, at 2:00 a.m., she didn't answer. Brandy was the type of person who kept her phone glued to her at all times. As such, he knew that if she didn't answer, it was purposefully done. He immediately dialed her number right back. Voicemail again! He pulled off the road and sent two back-to-back text messages. He waited for a response to either. Nothing. He headed home, angrier now than when the two of them had their confrontation on the phone the previous evening.

The Roots of Infidelity Go DEEEEP

Once home and settled down on his couch, he contemplated doing a pop-up at her home. He dialed her number once more. By this time, it was 3:00 a.m. No doubt, she had at least **looked** at her phone in the last hour. *"If she were as mad as she was earlier, she wouldn't have engaged in a texting conversation,"* he mused.

At 3:15 a.m., he was filled with rage and decided to make the trip to her house. As he made his way through her neighborhood, he remembered that if she parked in the garage, he wouldn't know for sure whether or not she was home. If anyone *else* were there, he would know because they would **have** to park outside.

As he approached her house, he noticed an SUV parked in her driveway. He couldn't pinpoint where he'd seen the Chevy Tahoe before, but he knew it didn't belong to any of her girlfriends. He parked a few houses away and began blowing up her phone to see if she would answer. On the third call, her phone went straight to voicemail.

Pat instinctively knew things were about to get out of hand. His temper was bound to take him to a place he tried so hard to avoid. Full of hurt and anger, he pulled up directly in front of her house, climbed out of the car, approached the door, and incessantly rang the doorbell. No answer. He laid into the doorbell again. Still, no answer.

Brandy must not have thought all the way through whatever dirty deed she was doing. The way her door was positioned, if someone (like Pat) went through the trouble of standing on the door seal, one could look into the small window on the front door and see clear through to her bedroom door.

He saw her bedroom light turn on and, in that moment, there was nothing that was going to stop him from getting her to either answer the door **OR** have her door kicked down off the hinges!

When he heard the lock turn, he was in for the surprise of his life: **David answered the door as if he lived there!**

"What's up?" David asked, irritated at the interruption in his pleasant evening.

The Roots of Infidelity Go DEEEEP

"Where the hell is Brandy?"

David opened the door all the way, and there she stood in her short nightshirt—and obviously nothing else underneath.

Pat is a prideful man. His eyes started to water, but there was no way he would allow a single tear to fall, especially in front of another man. He stood there, frozen by the shock of the scene. David turned to Brandy and said, *"Deal with this,"* as he walked out the door and to his car.

With his heart in the pits of his belly, Pat did what most would do when seeking answers: asked a million questions while obviously having the answers. Brandy, also prideful and selfish in many ways, stated that she had nothing to say and would not take the time to explain. Brandy knew there was nothing she **could** say. What was the sense of telling Pat something he had clearly seen with his own eyes?

Pat heard Joseph's words in the back of his mind: *"See the forest for the trees."*

With both of his hands balled up into fists and a strong desire to slap the taste buds out of her mouth, He told Brandy about herself. He read her up and down and told her how lowdown and grimy she truly was. *"All you had to do was be 100 with me. I gave you more than one opportunity, yet you chose not to be honest."*

Brandy grew more defensive with every assaulting word that flew out of his mouth. *"I do what I want, Pat. I sleep with whoever in the hell I want to sleep with. I don't owe you anything, not even my honesty. So, would you please leave my damn house?"* Before she turned to shut the door, she added, *"If you wouldn't act like such a bitch, you probably wouldn't have to worry about me being with another man."*

THAT was Pat's last straw on the camel's back!

He grabbed her by the neck, pushed her in through the door, and threw her across the floor. She jumped up and punched him square in the face. Both were blacked out in rage, fighting like two guys on the block. To avoid punching her back, Pat kept pushing her down to the floor every time she advanced. Trying to get her to stop

The Roots of Infidelity Go DEEEEP

was like telling a bull to stop charging; she didn't understand a thing. She kept swinging as if she was fighting a total stranger. When he pushed her down for what he knew was going to be the last time before he left, her head hit the stairs.

Stunned to silence and immobility, tears began to fall from her eyes. That fight took her to a place she vowed to never go to again. Pat saw in her eyes that she was truly done with him. There was nothing he could ever say to make it right. His apologies seemed only to make it worse, so he left.

Fifteen minutes into his return trip home, Brandy sent him a text:

"Your things will be in the trash."

"I don't care," he replied.

Frustrated, hurt, and at a loss for words, Pat found himself angry with the outcome of the altercation. Brandy's wrongdoing had somehow been turned around as if he was the one at fault.

"Let your conduct be without covetousness; be content with such things as you have. For He Himself has said, "I will never leave you nor forsake you."

Hebrews 13:5

THE OTHER SIDE OF THE HAND

When Pat arrived home, he noticed a DM (Direct Message) alert on Instagram. *"Hey! It's Jules. It was a pleasure meeting you tonight. I'm not sure why we met, but it was nice nonetheless."* Torn on whether or not to reply, he set aside the thought for a moment and headed to the bathroom. It was then he noticed the results of the physical altercation with Brandy: a swollen face! He stood peering at himself in the mirror for what seemed like an eternity. He allowed the tears to free fall. In his heart, he knew he should have stayed at home and accepted the night for what it was. He **knew** that going to Brandy's house would be *trouble*.

Unsure of what the new day would hold, he was confused about what to do next. Brandy had his heart in her hands — more than she could truly know. Pat prayed a prayer that many others have when in crazy situations:

"God, if you fix this, I promise to do better. **Please fix this!***"*

~~~~~~~~~~

On the other side of town, Brandy was upset with herself, too. *"How could I have let that happen?"* she asked herself. Taking a moment to replay everything in her head, she pondered over what move to make next. For her, the **easiest** choice would be to cut her losses on both ends and move on.

As it stood, she had a full plate. She was battling family issues with her mom who had been ill for some time. Having to tend to her mom and juggle her personal life, she was without room for any extra "stuff".

Even though she enjoyed the sexual experiences she and David had, she didn't want to be with him for a *lifetime*. She was physically attracted to him, and the sex was phenomenal, but she wanted and knew she deserved more than what he had to offer. She needed someone who would provide what she needed mentally, spiritually, **and** emotionally.

Those attributes rested with Pat!

Still…

The Roots of Infidelity Go DEEEEP

The sex with Pat was 'good enough'; however, there was something about him that didn't sit well with her. He had a scary past as it related to how many women he had been with. Of course, the two of them used protection. That wasn't the issue. The issue was that she knew at any given moment, they could be in a room with three or four of his old flings—and she would be none the wiser.

Truthfully, Brandy felt that Pat was too good to be true. He always made every single day all about her. He ensured she wanted for nothing. He was that guy who could wear a suit today and represent the business world like a superstar; the next, he could wear Timberlands and represent the hood…like a superstar. He was the perfect guy for her in so many ways. Pat had that "it-factor". He had it going on!

~~~~~~~~~~

Brandy remembers a time when…

One time, Pat picked her up for a dinner date. Being the gentleman he was, he rang her doorbell (versus announcing his arrival by sitting in his car and beeping the horn). When she opened the door, there he stood with 32 long-stemmed tulips—her favorite flower! Thirty-two represented her upcoming 32nd birthday, which was three days away.

They went out to dinner that evening. What took Brandy's breath away was that as soon as they walked into the restaurant, every person knew they were there to celebrate her birthday. They greeted her with so much love and the service provided was simply divine.

After dinner, she just knew the night was over. Much to her ultimate surprise, as they exited the restaurant, a helicopter awaited them. As they walked to her waiting "chariot", she was in tears. *"How did you know I've always wanted to take a helicopter ride over the city at night?"* she asked.

"I pay attention, my love. I remember you telling your mom your desire to do this."

*"That was a **long** time ago. I was on the phone with her when I said that!"*

"Yes. I know. I wasn't listening in on your conversation, but when you walked into the kitchen

The Roots of Infidelity Go DEEEEP

*that day and whispered that to your mom, my instincts kicked in. I **had** to make this happen for you."*

They take flight, and the route the pilot took had her over-the-top full of joy. They flew over every area of the city that held significance in their relationship: where they first met, first kissed, had their first dinner, and lastly, where they decided to make their relationship official. To make the night that much more special, Pat arranged for a firework display at each location. How he pulled **that** one off, she had no idea.

"Why are we celebrating my birthday today? You know it's not for another three days!"

He replied, *"You won't **be** here in three days. I've arranged for a few friends and us to go out of the country for your birthday"*.

Brandy was speechless.

As the magnificent night was coming to a close, Pat took her to one of the nicest hotels in the city. The room he chose overlooked the city with a special twist. In the distance, overlooking the river was an illuminated sign that reflected off the water. It read: **Happy Birthday, Brandy!**

Before she could catch her breath, he came up behind her, clinched his hands over hers, and began kissing her neck. He slowly undressed her, kissing every part of her body. He grabbed her tighter and tighter with each planted kiss. He rubbed her all over, squeezed her firm ass in the palms of his hands, and lifted her up onto the edge of the 12-foot high window pane. Slowly, he slid her up and down on top of his pulsing member. Passionately making love to her, he walked with their bodies entwined over to the bed. He gently laid her down on her back, never missing a stroke. Moving slowly at first, then building into a crescendo of sweat and love that was remarkable, she knew in that moment: It was all about her.

Unable to control herself for one second longer, she dug into his back with her nails, allowing her body to speak to him. Moans turned to screams of pleasure. Biting her bottom lip at the height of her climax, he drew her close to him as they both labored to catch their breath. Neither wanted to be the first to move, so Pat took the initiative. He cradled her in his arms and carried her into the shower.

Standing there with the water running down her back, Pat began to lather up the washcloth. Brandy looked at him, confused. That look quickly diminished when he began to wash her from head to toe.

Who would have thought that something as simple as the way he bathed her would cause her to look at him differently? He washed her with so much care. After rinsing off all of the bubbles, he knelt down and tasted her yummy goodness. As the water dripped off of his head, Brandy rubbed it with the gentlest touch. Having never experienced that type of intimacy in her life, she was left drained with the highest level of ecstasy ever known.

The next thing she recalled from her night of passion was waking up and Pat bringing her breakfast in bed. ***What a memorable occasion!***

~~~~~~~~~~

Enter in the events of the night. Truth be told, Brandy was torn. Although Pat had so much good in him, there were so many other factors to consider. A major issue was her inability to talk to him about her feelings. It was always a daunting task. Far too often, she found herself stuck. Sure, she played her part in the trials they faced, but that didn't mean she shouldn't be able to talk to him, right?

She attempted to write him a letter regarding her distrust:

"I don't know where to start. On one hand, part of me says to leave it alone and let it play itself out. On the other hand, the other part is telling me to be transparent. I didn't think it would be this hard just to talk to someone, but you make it difficult (to say the least), especially when it comes to particular topics. I don't think you understand how challenging you have made this situation. I am having some of the same feelings I had when I was with my ex.

"For starters, I should have never looked in your phone. I always say, "If you go looking for something, you will find it." *Me going through your phone forced you to deal with the issue when truth be told, you weren't ready. You were content*

The Roots of Infidelity Go DEEEEP

with playing both sides in your past relationships (not playing in a bad way…just dealing with two at the same time). That scares me. That keeps my wall up, although you can't see that. I see it in you. You appear to know what you want, but the problem is that you have trouble letting go of what you don't want — which is where the problem is for me.

"While I know I care about you a great deal, I feel as if I'm willingly accepting your intentions. I believe that adage that states, "Once a cheater, always a cheater." *It's a difficult position to be in.*

"You're likely asking where all of this is coming from. Well, specifically-speaking, the answer is this: your actions. When I watch you, you seem preoccupied. When I lay next to you at night, you're very guarded with your phone. I can't put my finger on exactly what it is, but it's there.

"At the end of the day, I'm at a place where I know what I want now. What I'm trying to say is that you can't hide what's inside of you. You don't know half of what I feel when I think about it. I know I have my issues to deal with. I try to work on them daily."

Feeling frustrated by showing her hand fueled her anger. *"I hate him,"* was all she could think about. Angry that he put his hands on her, she knew she didn't want to live that type of life. The last relationship she had was violent. In her mind, she knew what her heart desired; yet she (again) was torn because she refused to give any man the idea that putting his hands on her was okay.

As she sat there going over her thoughts and replaying the events of the night, her phone rang. It was David! Knowing that he, too, wanted to argue, she didn't answer.

A few minutes later, a text comes through:

"Brandy, you hurt me! I thought I was true to my word. I made it all about you and only you. I didn't go to your house to fight you. I did a terrible job of controlling my anger. For that, I am truly sorry. However, I am not sure how to deal with what took place. I care about you deeply. In all honesty, I am in love with you. For what it's worth, what we had was real to me. Take care. Pat."

Filled with a plethora of emotions and not allowing herself to give in to her prideful ways, she didn't respond. In her mind, responding would make her look weak. She refused to give any man that much of her.

The battle within herself continued. She knew what was done wasn't cool, but what could she say?

She bit the bullet and replied:

"Love doesn't hurt. You should have never put your hands on me."

That reply was going to have to be good enough. She quickly turned her phone on silent. Mentally, she was done for the night.

At daybreak, she grabbed her phone, expecting a message or two from Pat. The only message she had was from David. *"So, that's what we're doing now?"* Unsure how to respond, she set her phone down and said nothing.

Still upset about what took place with Pat, she called her mom to get her mind off of it all.

~~~~~~~~~~

Pat, on the other hand, responded to Jules. He told her it was a pleasure meeting her as well. Not wanting to be rude, he kindly explained that he would be taking a hiatus from social media for a few days. He simply wasn't ready to address his attraction to another woman. Rather than deal with it, he brushed it off as casually as he knew how.

Sitting on the couch, he began to reflect:

Growing up was hard for him. In fact, what many viewed as him 'having it all together' was a façade of having as many women under his belt as possible. To him, having women was the same as rich people having money. Many won't understand his logic, which prompts those who don't to ask, "Why do people cheat?" If they knew the answer, he was sure people would do things differently. As for him, he hated how women felt entitled to dish out the hurt. In response, he hurt himself in many ways. Of course, he didn't do it intentionally. The things that others didn't understand about relationships and infidelity were the problems.

He used to find solace in a drink here and there. In the beginning, the pains were dulled by the liquor, and all in his world was okay. Then, it got to the point

The Roots of Infidelity Go DEEEEP

when one drink turned into two…and two into many. That saying, "Drunks and babies tell the truth," was freeing. Being able to say and do whatever he desired while under the influence was a necessary outlet. He appreciated the idea of being able to operate without consequences—outside of the obvious hangover the next day, all the while telling himself he would never drink again…until the next round or two.

While Pat ponders his life, Joseph woke up to his new 'norm'; thinking of his life after masking his reality with drinks, women, and the late nights.

"Go to the ant, you sluggard! Consider her ways and be wise."

Proverbs 6:6

The Roots of Infidelity Go DEEEEP

TOUCHING THE SURFACE

It appeared to never be enough for Joseph. Partying, drinking, the women…things didn't seem right with him.

As many of you know, gluttony is the idea of having food or alcohol in excess. Now, one might ask, **"What in the hell does that have to do with cheating?"** You are correct if you said, *"Eating or drinking too much has nothing to do with one's actions with someone outside of a relationship."* However, when there are issues that go unaddressed, people seek to deal with them in different ways.

Have you ever heard of 'stress-eating'? The same goes for consuming alcohol as well. Have you ever thought about or known a 'nice drunk'? Or, better yet, a drunk person who is **NOT** belligerent? That doesn't touch the surface, though.

In this story, there was a reason Pat and Joseph connected. Both dealt with some form of infidelity. For Joseph, there were many reasons he chose to cheat. What's interesting is that many don't take the time to think their way through their deeply-rooted issues.

For example, lust is seen as an intense longing. It is usually thought of as an intense or unbridled sexual desire. That desire leads to fornication, adultery, rape, bestiality, and other immoral sexual acts. However, lust could also mean a simple desire in general; thus, lust for money, power, and other things are sinful as well.

Too often, people play with lust as if it's just an emotion or feeling. This particular sin, in my opinion, happens to be what I think is the most dangerous. For so many reasons that people wouldn't dare share, this one right here is heavy. For starters, when you are sleeping with your mate, how sure are you that he or she is thinking of you? The mind is such that no matter what your mouth says, no one (besides God) can ever know your deepest thoughts. All too often, when someone mentions a tall, dark, and handsome man or a 36-24-36 woman, you have a picture in your head of what that person looks like…***to you***. If I were a betting man, I would bet that more than half of you don't picture the one you're with. It's those inner thoughts that ultimately get us caught up in certain situations we know we should not indulge or entertain.

Lust is something that derives from the mind. The Bible states, *"As a man thinks, so is he"* (Proverbs 23:7). At one point in time, we have all heard a rendition of that passage of scripture. Digging deeper into the phrase, it is about having your mind made up of what you think you want or what you think will "do it" for you. We lust after worldly things almost daily. For example, there was a new cell phone or car you just had to have. You waited in line or until it was officially released and did whatever you could to get that very thing. The first few days of having it, you play with it day in and day out, getting familiar with it. When you feel you have gotten the hang of its use and purpose, you use it to the fullest of its capabilities.

What's the difference in lusting after a man or woman? Much like a new relationship, you engage in it day in and day out. Time goes by, and the relationship gets dinged up a little bit. You patch it up the best way you can and try to bring it back to 'like-new' status, but deep down inside, you know it's not new. Sure, you make it pleasing to the eye so that when someone else looks at it, it will be appealing to them. Little did you know, you have created a chain reaction.

Follow me here...

You dress that thing up with a new phone case or shiny rims all the way around. You even make it look good on the inside. You do everything you can to keep it looking brand new. Over time, the interior begins to look dingy or moves a little slower than when you first acquired that "it". One or two years go by, and you see the next newest version that's about to be released. Rather than keep what you have, you lust after the newest version. Before you know it, you have traded your old one for the newest model, failing to realize that you have now gotten deeper into debt. So what that the newer version has a few more bells and whistles! Inside, it still operates the same.

Those examples are likened to how we treat our relationships. *__Stay with me...__*

Very few men can detach what they see from what they have. Picture this: A man sees a woman walking into the room, and she is sexy as hell. Then, she starts to move as if no one else is watching. She grabs the pole and begins to dance

The Roots of Infidelity Go DEEEEP

in a manner that has him wanting to grab her by the waist and give her what he thinks she is asking for. The very thought of her big lips, breasts, and ass has him all over the place. In the midst of his arousal, his phone vibrates. It's his significant other. He plays it cool and, when he makes it home, he breaks her back out. In all fairness, he may not necessarily be envisioning that actual woman at the club; however, he damn sure is thinking about the way she moved!

"Beloved, never avenge yourselves, but leave it to the wrath of God, for it is written, "Vengeance is mine, I will repay, says the Lord."

Romans 12:19

The Roots of Infidelity Go DEEEEP

JOSEPH'S HAUNTING MEMORIES

I'm sitting here asking myself "Why?" **Why do I continue to act like the shit doesn't bother me?** *The bigger question is:* **How did I allow myself to be in the situation yet again?** *The sad part is that it appears the only way she will feel my pain is to experience my pain. No matter how I try to articulate my feelings, I am dealing with an individual who simply cannot relate because she has never experienced this thing from my perspective before.*

The laws of street life suggest I put it in her face, just as she puts it in mine; yet, my overwhelming love for her won't allow me to bring her that pain. Hence, both directly and indirectly, I feel and look like a fool. Could it be that she is that selfish? Did I lay a foundation of making her feel that I won't leave her, no matter what she did? Either way, the long end of the stick feels like it is shoved up my ass.

Old emotions are starting to flare up. I want to go completely **OFF**, *but then I start thinking about what takes place after I do. Is it worth it? My heart says "Yes!" But my mind… It says,* **"Keep it moving, Bro."** *I am far too old to play the merry-go-round games. I am far too hungry to live an honest life, but then I am looked at as a weak man or pushover!*

*Lord knows I am **FAR** from that. Then, the other question arises: If she truly loved and respected me, would I be dealing with this? The days of being considerate are coming to a head for me. Even steel breaks when extreme heat is applied. I feel my blood boiling internally.*

I still think about the lies you've told. Sincerely, I am hurting! I remember it as if it was yesterday when an anonymous number called your phone. I know I have seen that number before. You didn't answer. So, to have that same number ring your phone at 1:30 in the morning, I knew you couldn't say it was a relative or a friend in need because you didn't answer. Fighting the urge to pick up and answer the phone, the wrath inside of me wouldn't "just let it go". I answered the phone and said nothing. What I heard on the other end was shocking. "Hello? Hello?" a man replied to the silence. I clicked 'End' to disconnect the call.

*The extreme heat had been applied to my heart. My blood was **boiling**! I quickly tried to figure out how to make sense of my next move.*

Do I address it? Do I just leave? What to do?

The Roots of Infidelity Go DEEEEP

*Your phone rang **again**. It was at **that** point I made up my mind that he was clearly someone who felt he had the right to call you whenever he felt like it.*

I answered again without saying a word. "Are you at the gate?" he asked. I lost it! **"Who in the hell is this?"** *I screamed. Now, he's quiet – which further let me know he knew nothing about me. To think, I gave you chance after chance, and you still do this to me? To make matters even worse, you attempted to play on my intelligence by saying you have no idea who it was that called!*

Sidebar: The most interesting thing about this type of situation is how often it happens in relationships. When you look at it from both sides, you start to see how deep the problems you have with your significant other truly are. The guilty party finds himself or herself trying to figure out how they got caught slipping. No doubt, a rewind to a few hours prior with an opportunity to say, *"Don't call me; I'll call you,"* would have been wonderful!

As for Joseph, he finds himself sitting back replaying every situation that led up to that moment…

Do I fight for the relationship or do I continue to make myself look stupid? The most hurtful part of this process is not being made a fool; it's being made a fool because I was the last one to find out what was happening right under my nose. She didn't have enough respect for me to protect from her selfish ways. After all, she went so far as to bring other people into our lives on far too many occasions. So, now, not only am I a fool; I am a dumb ass fool who has been embarrassed!

*This cannot be love. It's definitely not right. There must be more going on than what I now know is going on. Going through the motions has become a habit that has us trapped in a weird place. It feels like I am the only one fighting for **US**. The world around us has brought so much into the idea of disarray being the 'new normal'. Good things no longer seem healthy. Everyone has ulterior motives. No one is being transparent about their truths. The slightest shift in any given day compounds the problem.*

You complain about me not talking to you, yet you have built up a wall so high, every time I try to conquer it, it's as if you are standing at the top waiting to throw rocks to knock me right back down. I can't help but wonder if I am the problem or simply not the

The Roots of Infidelity Go DEEEEP

man your heart desires. Either way, this is a very bad space we are in – and I don't like it.

I find myself wanting just to blurt out everything I'm feeling and suffer whatever consequences come. What causes me pause is when I think about how ignorant you become when you retaliate. Please don't take 'ignorant' as me talking down on you. Rather, I'm referring to the defensiveness you display. You have continued to hold on to your past experiences, which have truly shaped your thoughts about me. Ultimately, they are hindering you from truly embracing the love I have for you. You hide behind your anger, inability to sit still, and impatience. Your need to be seen and heard all the time causes you to miss what is right under your nose.

We have all been given the power of choice. Each day when I awake, I choose to use actions to back up what my heart is trying to yell at you. I know you love me, but the question remains: Is it really love or do you only love what I have to offer you?

Wait. Wait. Wait. Before you allow your defensive nature to overtake you, I clearly know you are capable of doing for yourself. You don't need me, and I'm aware of that. I am also aware of how I make your life easier in ways you don't see because those things are being worked behind scenes. Still, you have come to depend on them. For example, you know that no matter where I am or what I am doing, I will stop to answer your call. The very vibration of my phone ringing or a text from you stops me dead in my tracks. My heart beats a little faster in preparation for what you need from me in that moment. In your mind, your request may be simple. Are you going to cook dinner tonight (for example)? You have grown used to saying **"Joseph…"**, *and before you have time to think about it, it's done, or I'm there.*

What you don't take into consideration are the things I've had to adjust or maneuver around to ensure your needs were met. I have driven more than 100 miles per hour to reach you. Why? Because when you came into my life and I knew you were the one for me, I vowed never to allow you to want or wait for a thing. I desire always to show you that life has produced someone just for you; someone who will uplift you, spoil you, bathe you, and never let anything come before you.

Of course, it is the foundation I laid. I am proud of it, too! You don't see how you have become accustomed to the things that prove you're special to me. As such, you don't even consider if and when I have an issue. You know I won't ask you for anything

The Roots of Infidelity Go DEEEEP

nor make you feel as if you "have" to do anything for me, but it is always good to know you at least consider me and my thoughts.

Now what? Do I wait for things to grow progressively worse? Do I wait for God to come, tap me on the shoulder, and say, **"Hey, Joseph! Leave!"***?*

Sidebar: Think about it. In situations like these, the truth is that you find yourself in a situation of wanting in return what you have invested — minus all the hurt that came along with it. Of course, a simple apology is not always wanted. Why? Because saying *"I'm sorry"* and being a **sorry ass person** in the process contradicts the very idea of an apology. Still, there is something that is needed that acknowledges their wrong and the negative feelings that you now have. The crazy part is that when the apology comes, it can piss you off even more! You become almost insane as you live with the expectation that your significant other should give you something he or she cannot even give themselves: being 100% all the time. If that person was just real enough to let you know how he or she truly felt long before doing what caused you pain, the hurt could have been avoided.

"A sound heart is life to the body, but envy is rottenness to the bones."

Proverbs 14:30

The Roots of Infidelity Go DEEEEP

SORRY...NOT SORRY

Interestingly enough, while Joseph and Pat tarry with their own thoughts and relationship issues, Brandy struggles with thoughts of her past as well. Her fear of diving deep into a relationship is justified in many ways.

While sitting alone at home, she replays her previous relationship—the one that has caused her pause moving forward...

If you had even the slightest clue what my mind suggested I do to you... I gave you all of me! My ride-or-die commitment was all yours. In return, all you did was play games and gave me barrels full of bullshit. So many times, I thought about making you pay for what you did to me. You see, I don't like to play games because when I do, I play to win. If I indulged in the silly games you played, not only would I have purposed to hurt you; I would have done so to the point where the pain would have been irreparable. The sad part is you didn't see how your pride made you lose sight of who I was for and to you.

Let's pause for a moment here to "discuss" pride. Pride is a negative attribute that has stopped people from getting through things or accepting things for what they are. We give our all to others. In return, we desire loyalty. If something is "off", we should be able to articulate what we feel without an argument. The challenge comes when we are more connected to how we feel, so much so that we refuse to embrace what other people are feeling. We hide behind our words as if they are a mighty shield from the truth. We lash out in the most peculiar ways, hoping to get a reaction from the other party. In our moment of 'insanity', not only do we want a reaction; we also want to control it!

Take note: When you react differently than what is expected, you can effect change in that situation. It does **NOT** have to go downhill!

Moment of transparency: In times past, I have abandoned the very essence of me, all in the name of seeking a reaction. I've used words that I felt would soothe the recipient when, in fact, she wasn't looking for soothing words; she (rightfully so) sought believable **ACTIONS**. A mouth is capable of saying anything. A heart will often accept anything. One's mind, however, cannot process 'just anything' if there isn't a correlation between what a man thinks and does.

The Roots of Infidelity Go DEEEEP

John Maxwell is quoted as saying, *"There are two kinds of pride, both good and bad. 'Good pride' represents our dignity and self-respect. 'Bad pride' is the deadly sin of superiority that reeks of conceit and arrogance"*. Would you agree?

Back to Brandy's thoughts...

You were raised with a mentality that says, "Saying sorry makes you appear weak." As such, you tossed out "I'm sorries" like beads at Mardi Gras and continued doing whatever you wanted to do. Why even apologize? Damn. If you don't take the time to see my pain and feel my hurt, why should I care about what happens to you on this journey? Little did you know: A few simple words of comfort would have calmed me, but you were more concerned about 'looking weak'. How insane is THAT thought process? You openly claimed me as your significant other while preferring I look weak to others, yet you still chose to keep me close. In your efforts to not look weak, didn't we both appear that way?

I remember when I first found out about your other relationship — the one you claim was 'just a friend' because the two of you were simply occupying each other's time. You called it "conversation". I called it "wanting to hear another bitch's voice". The point is this: Why not call things exactly what they are? You were having a RELATIONSHIP with someone outside of what I thought was your REAL relationship.

I used to be excited about the possibility of loving you forever. I would do what I had to do to put and keep a smile on your face. You were my best friend, someone I knew I wanted to grow old with. You were like a dream come true! Falling in love with you was such a good feeling. I was wrapped up in your love and wanted more and more of you every day. How did all of that turn into missing you when you were in my presence? It could not be easily explained, but I knew what it meant.

I saw past your imperfections and your inability to love me as much as I loved you. When I looked into your eyes, I saw what most would say was a lack of love. Being the realist that I am, I call it: Not being the one you wanted from day one.

Every day, I tried to look past what you did. I lost friends in the process. I would often lose my appetite because that strong sixth sense would kick in and take a firm hold on me...that feeling of you being with someone else. Time after time, I tried to remove those thoughts; yet it seemed like every time I began to

The Roots of Infidelity Go DEEEEP

make progress, some unseen force would come and whisper, "Walk away."

Trying to understand the hold you had on my heart was a daunting task. It's crazy how much I can remember…and forget. I can hardly recall what I ate yesterday, but damn; those thoughts of you sexing another woman and allowing her to occupy your time would dominate my mind in the blink of an eye. Then, to find out the two of you did many of the same things you and I did! Was that to help you not forget the many lies you've told?

I was down with you. I damn near carried you when you fell off. Without hesitation, I would have fought the fiercest lion if I thought it would cause you harm. But you? You didn't have the decency to man up and keep it 100. Instead, you played on every insecurity I had, in particular, my inability to ride you like those whores in the strip club. To add fuel to the fire, you dared to tell me all the things you liked about them! The disrespect was **REAL**.

I gave you so many opportunities to be honest with me. I hated when you would nonchalantly ask, "Oh! What did you think? I was going to admit I cheated?" *For your information, my answer would always be "Yes!" Why? Because I would rather have the truth than live a lie.*

I remember when I begged God for you to change, even if it meant trying things that were unique to my nature. I was prepared to make that sacrifice. My only request? Don't cheat on me! Little did you know: Your actions played with my trust in God — and everyone else, for that matter. I often questioned God and His very existence. How could a Great God allow others to feel the pain that was ever-present in my mind intentionally? I didn't realize that same Great God was testing me. I failed miserably. Walking by faith is hard! The human condition makes us want to have the tangible and not wait on God. Of course, I'm still standing. Today, my faith is stronger. Still, there are times I want to ask: How can this be? I suppose you never realized you pushed me to my limit. It's amazing how far we take things when it comes to others' feelings.

There were obviously unaddressed and unresolved issues you had that stemmed from your past. You must have thought a stranger would fix them. You found yourself liking the other woman so much, the butterflies you used to have in the pit of your belly for me began fluttering for another. I noticed your nervousness as you prepared to spend time with her;

The Roots of Infidelity Go DEEEEP

always making sure you both looked and smelled good before stepping foot out the door – all the while telling me you're going to play ball with the guys. Why the deception? For an orgasm you thought was the best you've ever had? Or for the idea of selling that woman a false 'you' while I sat waiting and wanting those feelings we once shared?

*You were so damn comfortable around me, yet you couldn't tell me the real deal. How much more selfish could you have been? I reached out to you daily, asking what was wrong. Your reply? "*Nothing.*" I paid a hefty price for your inability to be real with me…and yourself.*

I remember like it was yesterday. You finally made it known that I didn't do it for you any longer. Confusion set it. You played musical chairs with your actions towards me. Hell, if it was that bad, you should have left a long time ago! Why did you stay? Again, I suppose you needed help with that, too. As you made your way out the door, all the bullshit you dished out was expected. You blamed me for every little thing wrong in your life. You constantly hoped for the worst when it came to us. It seemed as if you were always watching, waiting, and hoping I would mess up. At first, I couldn't put my finger on it. Now, it all makes sense.

*The interesting thing is that I know you will never find another like me. You may not regret your decision today, but sure as night will come, there will come a day when you will look back and wish you could turn back the hands of time. As for me, I know there is someone out there who will give me **ALL** that I need; someone who understands me without me always having to prove my worth…someone who will leave the drama to the reality TV shows, not our living room.*

The Roots of Infidelity Go DEEEEP

SOOTHING THERAPY

For Pat, he was having deja vu moments in many ways. While there were differences, foundationally, he was living a repeat of his marriage to his ex-wife, Whitney.

Many people never give themselves time to heal. We move on to other relationships without missing a beat, and before we know it, we have brought the toxicity from the former relationship into the new one.

Pat recalled all too well how not taking the necessary time to heal from his pains was a driving force behind his marriage's failure. The marriage lasted for seven years. From the outside, all appeared well—that was until both of them could no longer fake it. Their relationship was ripped apart from the roots after he caught her cheating. Deciding to make things work, they did what many couples do in times of crisis; seek advice or help from anywhere possible. Their help came by way of a counselor. Both knew it was a make it or break it moment for them.

Three sessions in, the major problem surfaced: lack of communication. Neither was honest about what they wanted or needed in the marriage. Both neglected the power of communication because they felt neither could speak their mind without repercussion. Gaining a better understanding of what true communication looked like proved to be their eye-opener!

Digging deeper into their issues, Pat couldn't help but be amazed at the growth that came from his interaction with the therapist. In particular, there were several instances where he felt motivated to do it all over again. He finally had the opportunity to understand Whitney even more, in light of their intercultural relationship.

Whitney's lifestyle while growing up was completely different than Pat's as it related to financial stability. As she listened to the struggles Pat had to endure, she was totally surprised to hear about his upbringing. Her facial expression turned from calm to concerned, as just for a moment, she felt the need to feel sorry for him. Embracing her concern, he quickly assured her that he was fine and could continue the conversation. Afraid to say the wrong thing in the moment, his assurance relaxed her. That was a turning point for Pat because it showed him a side of her that he didn't expect. Knowing she was truly a good person at heart, it was comforting to see how compassionate she could be. It was a great session!

Another memorable occasion was when they discussed how men should behave in a marriage. Not knowing precisely where she stood on that topic, it became clear early on that they shared some of the same views. Both believed that men should take care of the home and provide for the family. They also shared the same thoughts as it related to a man leading by example. It was nice to know they both embraced the idea that there were still some good men out there with traditional values, with Pat being in that number.

As they continued to communicate, Whitney's style of communication was mild-mannered and thoughtful. She was easy to communicate with because her posture was always one that showed she was fully engaged. She looked Pat square in the eyes and listened attentively when he spoke. Her level of interest was evident.

Looking back, one of the most notable differences between Pat and Whitney was that he showed his conviction through his facial expressions and tone of voice. She, on the other hand, remained neutral. At first, it was a cause for concern for Pat. Later, he came to appreciate her demeanor, as it relaxed him and allowed him to open up more.

There were times when the conversations during counseling were downright boring. In those moments, he found himself slouching in the chair — showing his disinterest. Unsure how his lack of positive posture would affect the atmosphere, he knew he needed to correct that behavior. With that at the forefront of his mind, he found himself feeling comfortable with some of the other tools taught to them without even realizing he was applying them. Being mindful of their differences in culture, both gained valuable insight into the other's upbringing, with Whitney's knowledge about people playing a significant role in how their lines of communication remained open for quite some time.

The Roots of Infidelity Go DEEEEP

When the topic of marriage was discussed, they were definitely in harmony with one another. It showed in their consistency in understanding the role each was to fill in the relationship. For example, even though both were exposed to different instances as it related to a man's role, neither allowed those influences to dominate their relationship or conversation. Pat knew many men who didn't take care of their families. Instead of saying things like, *"Such-and-such was a friend of mine who quit his job just so he didn't have to pay child support,"* he would simply state he felt some men could do better.

Sidebar: Being an effective communicator calls for you to step outside of the box and be open-minded. Be open to the reality of different people and differences in belief systems. In my opinion, this is the first step towards the goal of being an effective communicator. In addition to having an open mind, you must be willing to accept that people will not always agree with you. However, if you take the time to at least try to understand the other person's position (and vice-versa), tensions can be removed, and effective communication can take place.

Back to Pat's story…

Time progressed. Even with counseling, if 'that person' isn't "the one", it will come to bear. The positive effects of counseling lasted all of three weeks at best. It was about that time when Pat came to feel like lying next to Whitney was likened to lying next to a stranger…again. Sure, they communicated, but they lacked affection. It seemed as if they had a living arrangement that suited them as they made the best of their marriage. Still…

The disconnect was so apparent, it made being in the same room awkward. The saying **must** be true: *"You can hide keys, money, and phones, but you can't hide your feelings."* Given that, it wasn't long before things in their lives started shifting again. Pat wasn't the least bit surprised when he learned she was dealing with someone else. Let her tell it; he was 'just a coworker'. Better yet, "Quincy" was her 'work husband', as she so often jokingly stated. Their lunch dates to talk about work took a turn when she felt neglected (or so she stated). She was tired of Pat giving more attention to their children, his hobbies, and life in general than her. What she didn't know was that he was trying to keep himself busy to rid his mind of the many nights he wanted to be intimate with her and if she didn't say 'no', she opted to lay there physically — while mentally, she was in another place.

Whitney often mentioned her 'work husband' and what happened at work on any given day. Apparently, Quincy was a hot topic for her because even some of her family and friends knew more about him that Pat did. She was even bold enough to take Pat to a Christmas party where she introduced them to each other as 'my husband, Pat' and 'my colleague, Quincy'. People talk about women's intuition. Humph! As soon as the two men shook hands, Pat felt something was off. Then, Quincy had the nerve to carry on with a random conversation to turn the attention away from the obvious vibe that was flowing between him and Whitney. It was griminess at its best.

As the night went on, Pat found his heart rate increasing. Wanting to address his concerns, he knew he couldn't do so publicly for a number of reasons. First off, he wasn't about to cause a scene and embarrass either of them. He didn't have solid proof of her indiscretion. Secondly, he knew she wouldn't hear his pain. She would, instead, point out his insecurities—ones she brought on by telling lies in the first place. So, there he stood with his emotions all over the place, ranging from fear of the truth being exposed, fear of her playing on his intelligence, and fear of the unknown. Whitney was making a punk out of him, and he found it more and more difficult to face the foolishness of the moment. As the night bore on, she walked over to him and asked about the blank look on his face. He simply stated he had a headache. The long pause before she replied, *"Okay,"* let it be known that she was aware of the real elephant in the room. She told him she would be back after mingling more with her coworkers.

As she walked away, her head filled with trying to find a way to be alone with Quincy for a moment. She completely missed the opportunity to chill by her husband's side to alleviate his concerns. Neither were oblivious of the unspoken words that screamed louder than a yelling match between them. As a man, Quincy could have told her to deal with her husband for the evening—if he was so sure and secure in what they had going on. Instead, he fed off the thrill of knowing he

The Roots of Infidelity Go DEEEEP

could have Pat's wife whenever he wanted her. Pat searched and searched for his wife for 15 minutes. Neither she nor Quincy could be found.

Oh, the childish games we play… How many of you know that when you want something, you can make it happen in the blink of an eye? I suppose that's where the coined expression "quickie" came from!

For Whitney and Quincy, the hallway closet seemed like the best place. She couldn't wait to get her hands on him, and her moist panties spoke to that desire as he touched her. He grabbed her in a way that let her know: I do not have time to play, so be prepared to take all of me and take it fast! The tension that was heavy all night long was released when he entered her. With her eyes closed in obvious ecstasy, she felt every inch of him. What took five minutes (at most) felt like an entire love-making session. When they were done their dirty deed, one thing both knew for certain: They would be thinking about each other for the remainder of the night.

Quincy dipped out of the closet and immediately ran into another colleague. That was his out! In his mind, he was safe and sound. His absence was justified as the two of them stepped outside to smoke. Pat noticed him walking with his coworker but still didn't see his wife.

Whitney managed to sneak into the restroom unseen to clean herself up. Afterwards, she went and sat on the couch in the hallway and positioned herself where anyone could see she was on her phone. She hoped Pat would come looking for her. She decided to call her mom and made casual conversation about where she was. Fortunately for her, her mom was a talker. She knew her mom would want to talk about everything going on. Just as she'd hoped, Pat turned the corner heading for the men's room when he spotted her. Whitney's conversation grew progressively louder as she told her mom that they were going to be leaving the event soon.

You see, Whitney thought that by openly mentioning her husband's attendance with her at the party, he would know she was talking to someone that would help ease his obvious heightened concern.

The Roots of Infidelity Go DEEEEP

As Pat entered the restroom, he knew his thoughts were confirmed. He had a flash of anger that overcame him, one that led to tears. He knew the game she was playing with her phone long before that night. He also noticed how her routine shifted once Quincy came into the picture. She used to leave her phone lying around any and everywhere. Now, she kept it on her person all the time. The newness of her behavior did not go unnoticed. No longer were the children allowed to play games on her phone. The late-night texts she claimed were emails coming through, the constant Instagram logins, and the overwhelming number of times she laid in bed with her back turned to him while looking at her phone made it apparent that something was different. It was beyond obvious! *Who has casual conversations with their mom at midnight when, for the past few years, mom's pattern was the same; in bed by 10:00 p.m.?*

The ride home threw her off her game. As soon as they got into the car, Pat told her he had a good time. ***"Say what? Really?"*** she thought. He went on to mention how nice her coworkers were, including Quincy. ***"What in the world is going on here?"*** she pondered. He spoke about everyone equally to not raise any suspicions about his true feelings on the night. He knew if he kept her comfortable enough, she would continue being relaxed and would slip up somehow on her own. As they neared the house, he knew that to prove his point further, he would have to put her in a position to deny him any type of sexual encounter. He drove past the house and pulled into the parking lot of a bar both of them enjoyed.

Naturally, she asked why they were there. Just like a man with a plan, he put on his game face. *"Let's have a nightcap and listen to some good music before we head home. Nights like these don't come our way often, so why not take advantage of it?"* he boldly stated. Whitney had to go with the flow. What else could she say? The children were at the sitter's for the night, and there was no pressing emergency to pull her away, so she kicked off her heels, put on her comfy shoes, and said, *"Okay. One drink and then let's head home"*.

Pat felt she was distracted but had no idea as to the exact reason why. After all, this is what they did when they were kid-free!

Meanwhile, Whitney's head was clouded with how she was going to explain her long delay in texting him to tell him she made it home. But what could he say, right? Why would he trip when he knows his position in her life?

Pat kept a watchful eye on her mannerisms, but she operated like a pro. She walked in and did the same thing she normally did: stood beside him until the time came to order their drinks. Drinks in hand, they found a spot to chill and watch the crowd. On his next trip back to the bar, as soon as his back was turned to her, she hurriedly sent the text: *"Made a stop. Will be home soon. Had a good time. Can't wait to see you again. Long day. Sleepy. Wish I was sleeping next to you."* She knew by planting that 'sleepy' seed, it would be easier to sell the "I fell asleep" text the next morning. She quickly deleted the text and blocked his number. That way, she was sure his reply wouldn't come through while she was in the company of her husband.

The couple had their usual great time while hanging out at the bar. Finishing up their second round of drinks, he asked if she was ready to leave. Feeling a little tipsy, she replied *"Yes"* and they exit the bar. He grabbed her hand as they walked out, all the while going back and forth in his mind: What's my next move? He made it known that he's expecting to make love to his wife by gently grabbing her ass as they continued their walk to the car. As he opened her door, he told her how much he missed being with her and couldn't wait until they got home.

She knew what **THAT** meant.

Her mind started to race. She knew she couldn't tell him "No." She also knew she **just** had sex with Quincy. **Houston: We have a problem!** As she wrestled with those thoughts, she felt her husband's hand slide onto her thigh and his fingers creeping up to her still very moist spot. He hadn't done that since right before the first time they had sex. She knew he was about his business on that night! To her surprise, her body responded to that long, lost touch. For so long, she wasn't moved by his touch like that. To feel that again, she felt some type of way — in a *GOOD* way. Still, she felt a twinge of guilt overcome her because of what she had done just a couple of hours ago. Once home and in the garage, her heart began to beat faster and faster. She was truly in a pickle this time. She quickly walked into the house and made a beeline for the bathroom.

The Roots of Infidelity Go DEEEEP

Pat aggressively grabbed her by the waist and kissed her with passion. She tried to pull away and told him she wanted to wash up first. He responded by picking her up, placing her on the kitchen counter, and saying, *"**To hell with washing up!** I've tasted you after you've worked out, tasted you after a long day at work, and damn sure tasted you after we've been out for drinks. Nothing is going to stop me from making you grab my head while I taste you and your body tells me you are pleased"*.

Immune to her protests, he began tasting her as if it was his first time. In the back of his mind, he knew she did something she had no business doing. He told himself that when he finally decides to leave her, she **WILL** remember him. He grabbed her thighs and ate her out with unbridled passion. He was waiting for her to get so wet, she could feel it dripping down her thighs. He massaged her breasts while greedily munching her at the same time. He felt her body flex, and he **KNEW** he had hit that spot. She was so caught up in the moment, she didn't notice he had removed his pants. He picked her up off the counter, walked her over to the wall, and slid her down on top of his waiting, throbbing man piece. Starting slowly at first, they pick up the pace as he firmly grasped her ass in his hands. He pounded harder and harder until her moans turned into words. He knew that in a moment of passion, she always said what she meant — and he waited to see what words would escape her lips.

"I miss you," she said...over and over again. That wasn't good enough for Pat. He lifted her up higher and placed her legs on his shoulders. He goes in again, eating her aggressively. Both pain and pleasure swelled her growing clitoris. After some time, he walked her to the back of the couch and laid her over the edge on her belly. Her ass was positioned in a way that only allowed for him to enter from behind. Gripping the couch, she felt her hair being pulled as he entered her. He was in a zone by now, purposely beating up her spot so much so that her toes curled and her hands clenched the sofa just to keep her balance. *"Get it!"* she said. *"I'm about to cum, daddy!"*

The clock read 4:30 a.m. Whitney found herself waking up on the floor next to the couch. Trying to gather her thoughts, her body reminded her of the activities a couple of hours prior. With her swollen and still sensitive vagina, she made her way to the restroom to relieve and clean herself up. After doing so, she headed to the bedroom and immediately took notice that her husband was nowhere in sight. He wasn't in the living room, so she headed to the closet where a soft light was glowing from within. When she opened the closet door, she saw Pat looking at what appeared to be her phone.

"What are you doing?" she asked.

"Sitting here waiting on this private number to call you back. After you fell asleep, a private number called three times. I know no one would call at 2:00 a.m. unless it were an emergency…or something else."

"Something else like what?" she asked.

"Don't play my intelligence, please."

"Pat, I don't know what you're talking about."

"Of course, you don't," he sarcastically replied.

Knowing that an argument was looming, he handed her the phone and said, *"Things haven't been right with us for a while now. Tonight proved my point. What hurts me most is how you can detach yourself from what took place earlier at the party. While I don't know the specifics, I know you did something you weren't supposed to do."*

"What in the hell are you rambling on about now, Pat?"

He told her how much he loved her and because of that love, he is tuned in to her in ways she would never understand or know. He went on to explain that he knew her so well, he knows when she isn't being truthful and he damn sure knows she's not the 'mingling' type. *"When you left to go 'mingle', you* **had** *to know I was watching the room. Before you left, Quincy left the ballroom. When I noticed you weren't anywhere around, my anger started to rise. I thank God it took me 10 minutes to figure it out rather than five because five minutes before me seeing him walk out of that closet, I would have turned that whole place upside down. When I couldn't find either of you, I put on my thinking cap and reflected back in the day when I did something similar. The difference is that I would never give any other side chick the satisfaction of knowing she had one up on you. So, instead of leaving me alone in a ballroom full of people I didn't even know, you would have been better off doing what you typically do on any*

The Roots of Infidelity Go DEEEEP

*other night. You were too stuck on stupid to realize just how much you've been slipping the past few months. No, I did not witness Quincy sexing you down in the closet, but I know the two of you were in there. I will **NOT** give you the satisfaction of continuing to play with my mind, Whitney. I sincerely wanted to know if you loved me. That's why I made love to you the way I did tonight – like we used to do in the beginning. I sincerely wanted to wait a couple of days before talking about this issue to bypass the drama, but you were too sloppy with yours. You let this guy feel like he can call or text your phone any time of day or night. When you don't respond, he doesn't stop, which further lets me know what you have going on with him has been ongoing for a while now."*

He paused to gather his thoughts before continuing. He needed to be sure his message was coming through loud and clear.

"While you sleep, I toss and turn. When you talk on the phone or hide your text messages, my rage boils. There's no point in talking to you because you don't know how to communicate. You think that by saying, 'You don't have to be here,' you are making things better. Well, it doesn't. It's counterproductive! You want me to be something I'm not. I am who I am, but nothing I do for you is ever enough. I wonder how

*you would feel if I was not **HERE**. Would you even care, if only for a moment?"*

The silence in the room was deafening. He couldn't take it any longer. *"I will be back,"* he said as he left the house. As expected, she simply replied, *"Okay."* He knew she didn't care where he was going.

As he started the car, his intent was just to go for a drive and try to clear his head. The problem was that no matter how hard he tried, he couldn't rid his mind of the visuals that invaded that space. All he saw was her meeting up with Quincy. He also noticed she had on new lingerie—the same pieces he saw in the drawer the day before. It wasn't even about that fact as much as it was that she intentionally put them on to look sexy for him. She purposefully picked a fight, and he couldn't understand why she was being such an asshole. In hindsight, it all made sense now.

He thought about the many times she picked a fight, just to turn around and say that she needed a break and was going out with the girls. She failed to realize she had already set a pattern.

The Roots of Infidelity Go DEEEEP

She would leave the house all put together and return home carrying her shoes in her hand. When she walked in, he was so in tune with her that he was disappointed when he didn't receive credit for noticing how the bobby pin she wore on the left side of her hair when she left was now on the right side. It was all becoming too much for Pat to handle. Sure, he could leave; but where would he go?

Every friend he had was dealing with their own set of issues and wouldn't be able to empathize with his position, which held the utmost truth when it came to his homeboy and his girlfriend, Shelly.

> *"Let not the mighty man boast of his might…but let him who boasts of this, that he understands and knows Me…"*

Jeremiah 9:23-24

The Roots of Infidelity Go DEEEEP

SURPRISE, SURPRISE, SURPRISE!

Shelly lived and worked in California. Typically, she would return home to visit her boyfriend a few times throughout the year. Most recently, she went on a spree and would come into town once a month and stay for three to four days at a time.

Pat and Shelly's boyfriend were homeboys at one time. Pat told his friend that her sudden change in schedule seemed odd, but his observation fell on deaf ears. Pat was so well-versed in the cheating game, he often saw what the average person missed. He'd been there, done it **ALL** in the past.

During one of Shelly's extended stays, her boyfriend did a pop-up visit, attempting to surprise and smooth some things over with her. The GPS tracker on her phone led him straight to the Hyatt Hotel. Still not finding the location odd (because she stayed in hotels when she visited), he parked, went inside, and attempted to locate her. According to the tracking system, she had just arrived, so it shouldn't have been hard to find her still floating around the lobby. What he saw next raised his suspicion to the highest level: Shelly entered the elevator arm-in-arm with another guy! In that moment, he felt it was destiny's way of allowing him to catch her in the act.

Both the elevators and hallways were made out of transparent glass. One could be in the lobby and easily observe the room a person enters, no matter the floor that person was on.

Room #434!

He made his way up the elevator to the fourth floor. His heart was racing as if an ugly beast was chasing him. Before approaching room #434, he paused in the hallway to call Pat to tell him about what he just found out. Pat felt bad because it was he who encouraged his friend to save his relationship and surprise her with a visit. His friend expressed how hurt and angry he was, as he sought guidance on what to do next. Pat asked him to calm down as much as possible before knocking on that door, although admittedly, Pat wasn't sure even he could have taken his *own* advice in that moment.

The Roots of Infidelity Go DEEEEP

He put his ear to the door. Unless they had the TV or stereo on "extremely loud", there was no denying what was taking place on the other side. Shelly was caught. There was nothing more to say **OR** do. It was over between them. He walked away—no scene to be made, no words to be exchanged—and never looked back.

Since that day, Pat's friend has had a wall up and vowed to never again in life let it crumble—let alone fall. Obviously, he was **NOT** the person Pat could call to discuss his issues. After all, his friend detested the very ground *ALL* women walk on…

*"There is no fear in love.
But perfect love drives out fear, because fear has to do with punishment.
The one who fears is not made perfect in love.
We love because
He first loved us."*

1 John 4:18-19

THOUGHTS, THE OPEN ROAD, AND A GUN

Pat needed someone who would just listen and not say, *"I told you so!"* He was **NOT** in an 'I told you so' mood. He knew Joseph would understand, but he was often too busy traveling to sit still long enough to listen. Not really wanted to divulge his issues with any of his other associated, he took to the open road with his thoughts and no particular destination in mind.

After some time, he pulled up to a park where people used the paths for running. He sat there, listening to music…and crying. He was emotionally and mentally drained. He reached into the glove compartment, grabbed his revolver, and placed it in his lap. After verifying that all chambers were loaded, he put the barrel into his mouth and pulled the trigger.

Nothing. The big ***BOOM*** never came.

He forgot to turn the safety off! He started screaming loudly and repeatedly punched every part of the car that was within reach: steering wheel, dashboard, door, seat, and roof. When his rant was over, he asked no one in particular aloud, *"What in the **HELL** was I about to do?"* In that moment, he realized he needed to confront his demons head-on.

Pat called home, and Whitney rushed him off the phone. She didn't realize the call didn't disconnect. Pat heard her on her cell phone arguing with Quincy. Pat was so shocked by her side of the conversation, he couldn't miss out on the opportunity to record the argument. Of course, when confronted with the recording, she accused him of lying and said he had no such proof.

He replied, *"Instead of you being straight with me, you **STILL** choose to lie. You should know me well enough by now: I wouldn't say it if I couldn't prove it. Here you go. Listen."*

The replay of the one-sided recording started:

"I'm so frustrated with you. The turn-off is that you see it but won't do anything to change your ways. I hate that I love you, and I also hate that you are making everything about me and me alone. You say I force you to stay, but you seem quite content when

you're with me. You can't hide what your heart feels, despite what your mouth says.

"Last night was a perfect example of you starting an issue, and then once the other side of me shows, you call yourself being turned off by it. For the life of me, I can't understand how you say one thing but do something different. How many times have you said you are done dealing with me? The crazy thing is that you knew I was married when we met! You knew I had a husband, yet you continue to push up on me on a daily basis. You think you are the only one who's lonely? You have no idea what I'm going through over here! I'm very unhappy, and you are part of the reason.

"Apparently, I'm the only one who gives a damn! Why can't we talk about doing things that are going to make both of us happy? Hell, you think I want you staying there with your wife? Hell no! Somehow, you made it my fault that you're still there, even after I told you we could move in together and I would make sure we are taken care of. No, I'm not rich, but with alimony, child support, and the money I get from my dad's life insurance, I know we would be okay.

*"It's not about that, though! It's about **YOU** feeling some type of way at night. What do you think I'm doing? Laying up underneath him? Well, I'm not.*

*I told you before that I need to keep things the same so that he wouldn't notice anything different, but that doesn't mean we are have sex at every turn! You question me, but what about **YOU**? You are probably sleeping with **HER**! The best way to solve all of this is to move in together: you, your son, me, and my daughters.*

"Stop it. You know for a fact that if I turned my phone off at night, it would be a problem. Pat would definitely suspect something. You don't have to admit it to me, but deep down, you know that wouldn't fly. I so want to give you just a taste of what you give me just to prove my point.

"Whatever, Quincy. All you do is tear me down and tell me all the things I'm not. That kills me because you know I'm trying to be there for you. When no one else is there to talk to, I'm here. No one has your back as much as I do.

"In therapy last night, I was asked what makes me accept the b.s. on a daily basis. Aside from the abandonment issue with my dad, when I think about the b.s. I accept from you; my only answer is 'love'. If I didn't care about or love you like I do, I would have been long gone. I need you to let some things go. You

The Roots of Infidelity Go DEEEEP

have me up in here arguing with you, and I have a husband to deal with!"

The call and recording abruptly end.

Whitney stood there in quiet disbelief. Pat broke the silence. *"I'm the crazy one, right? You had two full-blown relationships going at the same time. Adultery at its finest! I'll be leaving and will call you to figure out how we will handle our daughters."*

"Hate stirs up trouble, but love forgives all offenses."

Proverbs 10:12

The Roots of Infidelity Go DEEEEP

FUNCTIONING IN BROKENNESS

As time passed, Pat and Whitney went their separate ways. He couldn't allow himself to forgive her. The pain was too much for him to bear. His unforgiveness robbed him of any chance at happiness, and he fell into a state of severe depression.

All along the way, so many people tried to warn him that something wasn't right with her. Wanting to prove them wrong while giving her the benefit of the doubt, he stayed in the marriage for all the wrong reasons, with the most significant that he didn't want to lose his family. But at what cost does one stay?

Once someone shows you who they are, believe them the first time. No doubt, most (if not all) people have played the fool at some point but to play the fool for the rest of one's life? That's not in God's plan for anyone!

If he was truly honest with himself, he knew that as a couple, they were incompatible in many ways. For Whitney, Pat was not her "type". She preferred dark-skinned men — and Quincy fit that bill. For Pat, he wanted someone who was versatile and able to adapt to any environment. She was a city girl with no 'life' outside of being bougie. She didn't want to "get dirty", and he wanted a woman that was free – in every sense of the word.

Someone who didn't feel she had to lock the bathroom door when she was on the other side.

Someone he could take 4-wheeler riding in the mud.

Someone whose family was just as free as she was.

While there is nothing wrong with the type of people Whitney and her family were, Pat was used to people being themselves and open to others doing the same. He must give credit where credit is due: She was a good mother to his beautiful children. Still, the two of them didn't work for reasons besides the obvious infidelity issues. He was a man functioning in brokenness, and he saw no way out of that conundrum.

The Roots of Infidelity Go DEEEEP

Roughly a year after his divorce, Pat met Brandy. He thought she was the most beautiful woman he had seen in a long time. They met at a sports bar. With the football season in full swing, it was the perfect time to focus on things other than the dreadful hurt of years gone by. He was sitting alone when he was approached by a group of ladies who asked if they could have the unused seats at his table. Without hesitation, he said, *"Sure!"* As Brandy was preparing to take her chair to join her friends, Pat asked her to stay. She gave him a shy smile, pulled the chair back up to his table, and sat down. The two of them conversed and laughed for a while. He learned that she was a mother to one boy and worked as a Pharmacist. He shared with her that he was in banking, which she was cool with. The evening got even more interesting as they discussed relationships: he, recently divorced; her in the middle of one. Her friends made it a point to mention that meeting Pat was just what she needed. Hell, they were attracted to each other! It was just what he needed, too!

Before too long, the atmosphere in the bar turned into one that resembled a nightclub. Her friends egged her on, telling her to stay with me as they made their way to the dance floor. She, on the other hand, didn't want to appear that she was cockblocking by not allowing other ladies to occupy his time. He insisted that she stay. The attraction between the two of them was almost overwhelming.

The two of them made their way to the dance floor to join her friends. From the outside looking in, one would have thought they were a couple as they moved in sync to the music, swaying from side to side rhythmically. When the music slowed down a pace, Brandy ordered a round of drinks for her and her friends. After that round, she ordered another. The next round came courtesy of one of her friends—and she even ordered one for Pat! He was totally enamored by that group of women! That **NEVER** happened in the clubs he frequented. His surprise was evident. One of her friends came over and inquired: *"Shocking, isn't it?"* *"Hell yeah!"* he replied. With the utmost simplicity, she stated, *"When you meet grown women, they act like grown women regardless of the scene."*

That was an *immediate* turn-on for Pat. He was prepared to take care of the bill for Brandy and her crew on the strength of that one friend, but all of them quickly assured him he was dealing with women who were obviously in a different league than what he was used to.

A few weeks pass, and one would think the two of them had known each other for years. After that initial meeting, they spoke every single day, multiple times a day. They went out every other weekend with friends and had the time of their lives—almost dismissing the fact that both had devastating past relationships. That's typically what happens when adults date. They recognize the other had a past, which should eliminate those childish behaviors. Unfortunately for Pat and Brandy, neither had taken the time necessary to address the issues from their pasts.

Brandy was a recent divorcee. Her ex was a man who had been physically abusive for years. Quiet as it was kept, she felt like he still had a hold on her, and she was fearful he would do worse bodily harm than he had while in the marriage. While married, they went everywhere together—unless he wanted to go out and hang with the fellas. To outsiders, his constant presence in her world might have looked "cute". The ugly truth was that he controlled every aspect of her life. Early in their marriage, he started selling drugs as a way to get them out of the hood. When he starting making that fast cash, other 'things' came along with it, including Brandy's increased loneliness. That was the hefty price she paid for living a life of luxury. She wanted for nothing and was the best wife she knew how to be. In addition to the turmoil surrounding her at home, she was also dealing with recovering from the mental abuse dished out by her grandfather. It seemed men always found a way to hold her hostage to their evil ways.

One particularly embarrassing situation occurred when Brandy and her husband went on a couples' trip to Las Vegas. While at dinner, the conversation came up about going to the club afterward. Her husband firmly stated, *"We can go, but Brandy can't."* While he didn't say it disrespectfully, it was clear to everyone in attendance that he held the controlling hand in the relationship. One of their friends mentioned to Brandy's husband that he was, indeed, disrespectful to Brandy and the rest of the group. That friend's husband shushed her by saying, *"That's how they rock. She'll be alright"*.

The Roots of Infidelity Go DEEEEP

Needless to say, that trip didn't sit well with Brandy. The relationship was made even more difficult—and the abuse continued until she was able to walk away once and for all.

"But love your enemies, do good to them, and lend to them without expecting to get anything back. Then your reward will be great…"

Luke 6:35

The Roots of Infidelity Go DEEEEP

STABILITY? WHAT'S THAT?

Pat and Brandy, with time, have decided to somehow make their relationship work after the fight they had. In the same breath, Brandy had yet to heal from the pains of her past. They both had glaring issues that remained virtually untouched and failed to recognize the role those undealt-with issues played into the difficulties they would face while trying to regain stability in their lives—both as individuals and as a couple.

Brandy was in the midst of trying to gain a foothold on her newfound freedom after her divorce was finalized three months into her and Pat's relationship. She still found herself easily-enraged when she felt as if someone (especially a man) was trying to tell her what to do.

For Pat, his trust issues rode shotgun on a daily basis. It didn't help that Brandy had a lot of male colleagues that she hung out with and spoke to outside of work. The dynamic between the two of them was beyond interesting.

What were they to do?

113

Well, like most people, they chose not to address the red flags that were waving wildly right before their eyes. The chose to, instead, continuing living their happy lives. It would have been too difficult and time-consuming to address their issues and help each other heal. Going on with their lives as if they have all the time in the world was the choice they made.

But those unaddressed issues and outside influences? Neither of them was consciously aware of how each negative situation they encountered played a role by mentally draining them, especially those of Pat's friends who were unstable with no desire to up their own game.

For Brandy, her circle wasn't much different. The ones who were stable were dealing with daddy issues and other situations that were unhealthy for anyone to be exposed to. One of her friends acted out by whoring her way through life, sleeping with almost every man she met within the first couple of days of meeting them. To further add to her whorish ways, it seemed like no matter where she went—grocery store, the club, church—all of the guys knew her.

The Roots of Infidelity Go DEEEEP

Slight pause here. If the word "whore" offends you, let's just couch the type of woman she is as 'one who likes to have sex, no matter who it's with'. Choose how you want to define it so that your blood pressure doesn't shoot through the roof and you feel as if you want to burn this book.

The point being made here is that Brandy's friend's looseness proved to be an issue for Pat because he was not able to understand how that woman's actions didn't flare up a cause for concern for Brandy. Instead, she would defend her friend by stating that the men were being just as whorish and that they're all adults. For her, it was "whatever floated their boats".

For Pat, he felt that **ANYONE** who slept with multiple people on a consistent basis displayed whorish characteristics—male or female—and it bothered him to the core.

What he didn't know initially was that Brandy's nonchalant attitude regarding sex was attributed to being molested by her grandfather as a little girl. She didn't have the protection of her father because he passed away when she was five years old. Her mother was on drugs and always in the streets, leaving her alone with the sexual whims of her grandfather. As such, Brandy had a lot of built of resentment for her mother and was regularly haunted by memories of her horrific childhood. Those thoughts shaped her way of thinking about men in general.

The Roots of Infidelity Go DEEEEP

HE MADE ME TOUCH HIM

Brandy's mom **REALLY** loved partying. It was during those times when the resentment for her mother grew exponentially. How could her mom ignore the signs? Was she *THAT* detached from her young daughter's well-being that she couldn't see Brandy was hurting both physically and mentally?

Brandy remembers when...

I cried and begged for mom to stay home. She had gotten all dolled up and said she wouldn't be gone long. We loaded up into the car heading for Aunt Jessica's and Uncle Ray's house. My unease wasn't attributed to my mom's need to run the streets. It was about all the things that took place while everyone was asleep that caused me distress.

Single for most of my young life, mom enjoyed hanging out in nightclubs or with friends more than she did spending time at home. I suppose she was trying to find someone she could call her own. It was normal for me to see mom with one man after another. One day, it was Robert; the next, Carl. Then, there was her best friend, "Uncle Charles". Of course, she didn't think I heard her and "Uncle Charles" having sex when they thought I was asleep. Even as a young girl, I knew he wasn't family. I also knew I couldn't say that aloud for fear of severe correction in the form of a slap in the mouth (at minimum) for my disrespect.

I used to spend countless hours at a time at my aunt and uncle's house. My cousins and I didn't have much in common. They enjoyed playing their video games; I enjoyed quiet time in front of a television. As such, the routine was set in place: I would often be alone, left to watch whatever cartoon tickled my fancy, while the rest of the household would be off in another room enjoying their family time. Family time; that was a foreign concept for me, but I longed for what they had. Typically, my mom would pick me up late in the evening or early the next morning after her night out on the town.

On this particular night, when my cries for her to stay home fell on deaf ears, my tears came from a place of fear. I was living a nightmare. I couldn't understand how bad things were happening to me and no one acknowledged my obvious turmoil.

You see, the week before, it was business as usual for my mom. She went out, and I went to aunt and uncle's house. I remember taking a bath and settling down on my spot on the floor to watch a movie.

The Roots of Infidelity Go DEEEEP

Aunt Jessica and Uncle Ray were sitting on the couch, and my cousins were almost asleep. Right before the movie began, my aunt said she wasn't feeling well and was heading to bed. She stirred my cousins and told them to get off the floor and into their beds. That left Uncle Ray and I – bright-eyed and bushy-tailed.

He asked if I wanted to sit on the couch. That was a rare opportunity for me, so I readily agreed to climb up there to sit next to him. As the movie played on, I found myself getting sleepy as well. He said, "Don't worry. If you fall asleep, the movie will be here when you wake up". Uncle Ray was an intimidating man, standing at almost seven feet tall with a muscular build. His presence demanded everyone's attention whenever he entered any room. I didn't expect to be the recipient of the attention he decided to give me, though.

As we sat watching the movie, he asked me to rub the inside of his thigh because it was sore. He grabbed both of my hands, guided them past his thigh, and placed them inside his pants through his open zipper. I remember shivering with fear. Somehow, I knew what he was doing was wrong. He pulled out his penis and forced me to grab it and stroke it up and down. As I did, it grew bigger and bigger. His enormous hand over my little ones expertly handled his throbbing member. Instructing me not to cry, he lifted my nightgown up past my hips, forced my legs open, pushed my 'Saturday' panties to the side, and forcefully touched me with his free hand. I was confused, scared, and unsure what to do. I hoped someone would have walked in to save me. That didn't happen.

The molestation grew progressively worse each time I was dropped off there. What started off as a rub and a touch grew into full-blown rape (if it walks like a duck…). *He forced himself inside of my tiny body, all the while telling me not to cry and not to tell anyone about our little secret. His constant threats to kill me if I told were just as real to me as Santa Claus was back then. The obviousness of my fear about those trips to their house went completely unnoticed. I couldn't understand how not a single adult didn't see my discomfort!*

The last time he raped me and left me bleeding profusely, I knew I had to do what I could to bring the abuse to a stop. Trying to figure out a way to tell someone without him killing me, I devised a plan: I left my soiled panties mixed in with my aunt's dirty laundry, hoping the discovery would trigger **something** *in her mind.*

The Roots of Infidelity Go DEEEEP

When my mom arrived to pick me up that night, I was certain someone would have found my underwear by then, and the topic would come up when my uncle wasn't around. As I walked past the laundry room on my way to greet her, I heard the washing machine going through a wash cycle. Before I could utter a word, my uncle casually stated that he washed a few of my things and that he could keep them there for the next time I came over.

That bastard washed my clothes!

Scared out of my mind, I never said a thing. Seeing how my mom interacted with him, giving him hugs and laughing it up all the time, made it even worse. I knew if I told, no one would believe me. Until this very day, no one except me, Uncle Ray, and God knows what happened on the other side of aunt and uncle's door.

"You were cleansed from your sins when you obeyed the truth, so now you must show sincere love to each other as brothers and sisters. Love each other deeply with all your heart."

1 Peter 1:22

CAUGHT UP IN WHAT IT ISN'T

To this day, Brandy holds resentment towards her mom for not "seeing" the pain she went through. Harboring those ill feelings all of these years later, she had a full plate. The issues she had with David and Pat didn't help.

Up to that point, Pat still had no clue what Brandy was dealing with. Allowing his mind to take control of his actions, he found himself in 'protection-mode'. Up went the wall that guarded his feelings oh so well. In that moment, Jules was the only one who could help him cope. Funny thing: Jules was also thinking about reaching out to him while having no clue about the depths of the issues involved in Pat and Brandy's relationship.

As time passed, Jules was left wondering just where she stood with Pat (she didn't know the depths of problems Pat and Brandy were facing). Pat, knowing he was playing with fire, went against his better judgment and messaged her. *"Hey, you!"* When she opened up her Instagram app and saw it was a message from him, she lit up. Excited to hear from him (and blinded by the fact that he had a 'situation'), she found herself emotionally caught up. He never tried to hide what he was going through, although he might have toned it down some when discussing the topic with Jules. He made it clear early on that he didn't want anything more than friendship with her. Still, she was caught up in the idea of what Pat and her **could** be.

As Jules sat on her balcony, she let her thoughts wander…

I can't help but wonder what he's doing. I mean, I know we're not in a relationship and can't be mad about the time we're apart, but damn; I haven't spoken to him in a few days. Of course, we had the conversation about him not wanting to date anyone right now, but I can't help that I care about him. He intrigues me in a way I can't explain. I want to talk to my friends about him, but I know it won't come out right. They can see my face lights up when he calls, yet I can't tell them anything more than, "I like his swag." *I see him from time to time for a short while. We have never spent a day together. We never go anywhere. If I'm honest with myself, we only hang out when we sleep together. I understand he's busy. I try to give him his space. But damn! I know what I feel. I can't believe it's been three weeks since I last saw him! I don't want to come off as desperate, but I am so sick and tired of being lonely.*

*Truth be told, he moves me like no one else does. The few times we had sex, he made me feel just what I needed. I don't want to be just his sex partner: I want to be **HIS** partner. I'm trying my best to be an adult about what we have going on. I would be there for him when he needs me, but he shuts me out every time. Hell, now that I think about it, he shuts everyone out!*

What am I missing? Is he showing me signs of what it really is and I'm not paying close enough attention? Or is he being 100% honest with me and I simply don't want to accept the fact that he doesn't want a relationship?

*Casual sex isn't casual for me. It's deeper than that. I am **NOT** in the business of having sex just to have sex. But damn, damn, **DAMN**! Even the sound of his voice makes my insides light up! When he smiles, he lights up the room. Where do I fit into his life, though? All of my friends tell me I'm crazy to be in a relationship like this, but they don't understand because they have yet to find the one who will make their heart flutter.*

I am at a loss right now. Oh, the things women do behind the power of the penis! When alone, sex toys are cool; however, there's nothing like a touch in the right spot from someone else. If he ever gave me the opportunity to be his, I would – without hesitation. I have no desire whatsoever to be with another man, although they are a dime a dozen. I suppose I am settling. I shouldn't do this to myself.

He called yesterday and said he wanted to come over to chill. Now, most women would take that as a cue that he wanted to have sex. That is not the case with him. He is so upfront; if what he wanted was sex, he would straight up tell me that. So, I waited…and waited. He was a no-show. Him and his damn work schedule! I guess time will tell where we're heading.

Let me place an author-pause in the story right here. It's time for some serious self-reflection.

Do you find yourself in a similar situation right now? If so, look at it for what it is and match that up with the desires of your heart. Often, we try our best to be understanding. For how long, though? At what cost to our sanity? Looking at it from different perspectives, we have to make hard decisions today to better our tomorrow. In this day and age, time is not on anyone's side; however, there are consequences associated with rushing into things as well.

Think about this: Let's just say you get into a relationship with someone after they made it very clear they weren't ready. What then? There have been far too many instances where women put themselves in situations that, in the long run, cost them their peace, happiness, and even their lives. And for what? The 'security' of a penis at home? In my opinion, it's not worth it. We cannot control what other people do, but we can control what we do and how we respond to situations that are presented to us. Let that last sentence soak into your soul.

Back to the story…

For the life of him, Pat could not understand the reason why Jules was so into him. As he tarried with whether or not the grass was truly greener on the other side, he remained oblivious to the fact that Jules had some heavy issues and cumbersome burdens. For her, anything that resembled "different" than her past was a way of escape. As far back as she could remember, she had been exposed to being cheated on and, as such, lacked respect for any man who even attempted to get one over on her.

Pat's honesty was refreshing — and a turn-on for her in many ways.

The Roots of Infidelity Go DEEEEP

THE TEMPTRESS HAS ARRIVED!

It wasn't that long ago when Jules confronted her dad for what he did to her mom…

"I know you cheated on mom multiple times. In fact, I know who she was, dad."

He was confused as hell and didn't know how to respond. In his mind, he thought his long-time mistress was a well-kept secret—at least one of which his daughter wasn't aware.

Larry, Jules' dad, knew when things became challenging in his marriage…

The time came for Larry to give his life to Christ. He knew that his wife wanted nothing more than a God-fearing man. He felt if he could pull it off long enough, maybe all the issues of his past would fall by the wayside. Very few knew of the inner demons he fought with on a regular basis; the good and the bad trapped in one body. He recalled the dear words from a wise man in ministry: ***"Fake it until you make it. Or, if you are going to Hell, why not go First Class? There is no sense in sitting at the back of the plane to Hell. Fly First Class and enjoy yourself!"*** It amazed him that he still remembered that ill "advice". He actually looked up to that man and all that he represented. From the pews, Larry had an appreciation for the way the man pronounced his words and how he could roll scripture off of the tip of his tongue with ease. Being a born-again Christian, how well-versed that man was amazed Larry—not to mention the amount of attention he received from the women in the church. That level of power was tantalizing to "Larry the Newbie".

The main purpose of his transition remained intact, though. If he could commit his life to Christ, he would grow closer in his relationship with Him and rid himself of the things that haunted him for so many years. Maybe, just maybe, he could get his marriage back on track and be a difference-maker in the body of the Christ after the scandals that rocked the church as a whole. *"Why not be the beacon of hope for others to follow?"* he thought. He didn't find it at all odd that he could trick himself into believing he was doing it for the right reasons.

The Roots of Infidelity Go DEEEEP

"Pastor, I really enjoyed your message today. I want to become involved in the church in some capacity," Larry mentioned after service.

"To God be the glory, my man," the pastor replied. *"Come see me after Wednesday night prayer meeting this week."*

It was then that Larry noticed his wife's stargazed look. He took immediate notice of how she looked at him in awe, and he couldn't understand why. As soon as they crossed the seal of their home, she was unusually kind to him. Her whole attitude was about doing anything and everything for him. It was a welcome change but quite unexpected.

When Wednesday came, she anxiously waited to see if he was going to ask about bible study. *"Had a long day at work?"* she asked. *"It was okay. However, I'm looking forward to bible study tonight. Do you want to join me?"* he replied. Before he could begin his next sentence, she had the keys in her hand. Off to church, they went.

All the way there, his mind was racing with thoughts of how he could best serve the church. He had a pretty good idea of what he wanted: to be a minister much like the iconic man who preached to his spirit-man from the pulpit every Sunday.

As God would have it, he became involved in ministry, and things seemed to be going quite well—so much so that he quickly found himself rise to the position of being the pastor's right-hand man. Nothing went on in the church without his involvement. During that time, he was the model minister. He stayed busy and didn't have time to think or focus on anything else. Things at home seemed to get better as well.

One day, while cleaning the church, a car pulled up. It was Sister Tina. She was one of those single ladies who always hung around the ministerial staff, was known for making her way both in and out of churches, and wore clothes that caught every man's attention. *"Hey, Minister Larry! How are you today?"*

"Fine, Sister Tina. How many I help you?"

"I wanted to ask if the adult basketball game will still be played since the weather is bad?"

"As far as I know, yes."

The Roots of Infidelity Go DEEEEP

Now, why in the world would she drive all the way there to inquire about a basketball game was beyond him. He could have taken a million guesses, but he didn't want to come to any rash conclusions. Lo and behold, her true intentions came to light in her next breath.

"Minister, I know this may be inappropriate, but I will only go to the game if you're going."

"Now, Sister Tina, I appreciate that. But what does me going have to do with you supporting the church?"

What she and many others saw in Larry was an upright, godly man involved in the church. What they didn't see was the 'old Larry' who recognized game from a mile away.

She flirtatiously chuckled at his response and said, *"I want to support my church, but I can't lie and say I didn't want to see you there."* She followed up that confession with a seductive look.

He quickly shut her down and thanked her for coming by. As she left the parking lot, he began to recall all of the things he heard about her and the way she could make any man consider stepping outside of his marriage — if not leave it altogether. Admittedly, she was eye candy but nowhere worth leaving his wife.

The day of the game, he caught a glimpse of her as she walked by. She made sure people knew she had arrived. Larry watched as man after man shot her lust-filled looks out of the corner of their eyes. The women, on the other hand, looked at her and thought, *"Look at that tramp! She barely has any clothes on!"*

He noticed his wife's piercing eyes looking dead at him, almost daring him to give her a second look. He had to make sure she didn't see the look he had already given the temptress with his sinful eyes. He couldn't wait for the game to be over so that he could leave and get those crazy thoughts out of his head. The entire ride home was spent with his wife talking about how inappropriate that woman was.

The next week at church, he needed to arrive early to prepare for the guest choir that was coming. They anticipated having an unusually large crowd in attendance. As he pulled up, he noticed there was a car already in the lot: Sister Tina's. Before he could get out of his car, she was at his window crying and asking if she could speak with him. Taken aback by her open display of emotions, he hurried her into his office. When they entered, he noted she was truly bothered by something. He asked her what was wrong and, crying her heart out, she explained she lost a close friend and didn't have anyone to talk to about her loss. As he handed her a tissue, she grabbed his hand and sincerely apologized for anything she has done to make him feel uncomfortable around her. Her touch did **NOT** help ease his growing discomfort in the confines of his office. Recognizing that was not the time nor the place to discuss something like that, he assured her all was well and instructed her to focus on feeling better.

When she bent over to grab something from her purse, he was blown away by her **lack** of undergarments.

"But he gives us more grace. That is why Scripture says: 'God opposes the proud but shows favor to the humble'."

James 4:6

The Roots of Infidelity Go DEEEEP

LEAVE THAT TITLE AT THE DOOR

For what it's worth, Larry truly did try (in his humanness) to do right by the position he held in ministry. He had good intentions — for the most part.

He recalls a particular counseling session where he spoke from a human (versus ministerial) perspective concerning two members…

Nine a.m. came faster than expected. Church service wasn't until 11, but the doors to the church and other preparations needed to be made. Larry, now a minister, was mentally preparing himself for worship service, as he knew that once he arrived, he would need to talk to Leroy, the Head Elder. Leroy was dealing with issues in his relationship — the kinds that many wouldn't believe were going on behind **HIS** closed doors.

A few weeks prior, as Larry was leaving bible study, Leroy's wife Octavia approached Larry. She was very distraught about the things that were taking place in her home. She mentioned instances of brutal verbal and physical abuse. Without showing just how shocked he was at the news, Larry listened with what he hoped was an unbiased perspective.

"He constantly tells me how fat and unattractive I am. I can't do anything right. No matter how many times I dress up for him or cook his favorite meal, he constantly talks down to me, making me feel lower than the dirt on his shoes."

She then shared with Larry the most recent incident that scared her nearly to death and left her wanting out of the marriage:

It was around 10:30 p.m. when Leroy returned home. He had the stench of bourbon on his breath. As he made his way to the bedroom, he grabbed and kissed her aggressively. She asked him to stop because she knew he was drunk. That prompted him to grow even more belligerent, talking to her as if she were a whore and not his wife of 18 years. It was the most degrading moment in the history of their marriage.

In an attempt to calm down an escalating situation, she said, *"God would not be pleased with you right now."* All the feelings she had for him and towards his ministry soon surfaced for exactly what they were when Leroy yelled, ***"God? Who cares what God thinks? If God was all that He said He was, why in the hell did he not change your fat ass into someone more appealing? Why didn't "GOD" show you how to please me, woman?"*** Fear crept into her soul. She couldn't believe those insensitive words departed from his lips! She knew about and tolerated his extramarital affairs, but **NEVER** in a million years did she think He didn't believe in God with his whole heart, mind, and soul!

He went on to tell her how disrespectful she was for bringing God up, and before she could see it coming, he slapped her so hard, her ears rang as she hit the floor. Trying to defend herself, she pushed him away. That only escalated his anger, so he grabbed her by the throat, lifted her high in the air, and started choking her. *"I will kill you, woman! Do you hear me? Don't you **EVER** disrespect me again!"*

When he let her go and she fell back to the floor, the tears that fell from her eyes were those of someone who almost lost their life. It was evident from that moment on that the nature of their relationship would be changed forever.

For what seemed like hours on end, she sat on the floor and cried. As Leroy started to sober up from the adrenaline rush that overcame him, he knew he messed up. *"Baby, I am so sorry. I'm sorry. I'm sorry..."* He continued to apologize, begged for her forgiveness, and blamed his behavior on the alcohol. *"I didn't mean anything by it,"* he said. The more he spoke, the more hurt and angry Octavia became. Leroy was fresh out of comforting words and excuses.

"Just leave," she calmly stated at first. Then, with a renewed boldness, she yelled, ***"Just get out of my house before I call the police!"***

He begged and begged for her to give him another chance to make things right. She wanted no parts of what he said. He went downstairs into the guest bedroom, locked the door behind him, and busted out in tears. He knew he had gone way too far this time.

Upstairs, Octavia finally gathered her strength to get up off the floor and climb into the bed. She eventually cried herself to sleep, while feelings of regret and physical pain flowed through her body.

As she tearfully recounted her horrific experience, Larry couldn't help but allow the human side of him respond. He simply suggested that she do what she felt was best for her. He was not about to dismiss her dilemma by telling her that God will fix their relationship. He kept his words sincere and real with her when he said, *"You didn't deserve any of what happened to you."* With Octavia's permission, Larry assured her he would have a one-on-one man-talk with Leroy.

Larry didn't let on that he knew about the incident, but the two men did plan to meet that morning. Leroy was scheduled to preach that morning, and in good conscience, Larry could not allow that to happen. Although the church bulletins were already printed and had Leroy's name as the preacher that day, Larry knew he had to switch things up in a way that wouldn't alarm the congregation or have them asking questions.

Sidebar: In addition to being nosy individuals, church folk can truly make things worse than what they are by making any one topic "the talk of the church".

As Larry sat in his office, the knock that came from the other side of the door let him know it was time. All titles had to be left at the door if the two were going to speak man-to-man.

"Good morning, Minister!" Leroy said cheerfully.

"Morning, Elder."

The elephant in the room was much larger than the room would allow. Larry didn't stall. He went right to task.

"Elder, what's going on with you and Octavia? Talk to me. Know, too, that this is not a conversation of judgment. Rather, it is one of transparency and what needs to take place to right the wrong for both you and Octavia."

Leroy was initially very timid during the conversation—not at all like the man who stood in the pulpit and preached the Word of God. He was very emotional and honest, stating that he felt lost and trapped in a world all alone. He didn't have anyone to talk to, so he used the opportunity to tell Larry about things in his home that showed how bad life was for him.

Leroy shared how he started to become distanced from his wife when the affair he was in grew progressively deeper and deeper. The longer it went on, the further away it pushed him from his wife. He also acknowledged that he knew he wasn't living by God's word with a pure heart, while the pressure to not cause a scandal in the church caused him even more heartache. Rather than facing his truth head-on, he found comfort in alcohol…and another woman. He admitted that he became active in the church primarily because it's what his wife and parents wanted for him. In an attempt to not let any of them down, he found himself trapped for many years, with no easy way out.

The abuse towards Octavia came by way of seeing what his parents went through. In his mind, his mom stayed with his father in spite of, so he expected nothing less from his own wife. His mother endured the abuse for numerous years after being married for over 40 of them; surely Octavia would do the same. He couldn't connect the dots and see how wrong he was for living in the shadows of his father.

As Larry listened to him pour his heart out, he began to see how unevenly-yoked Leroy and Octavia were because of their upbringing.

Octavia grew up in a single-parent household. Her mother, who was on drugs, left her with her dad at a very young age. By the time she was eight years old, her mom passed away from a drug overdose. Her father struggled to raise her, but spoiled her and treated her like a princess. As a product of that example, she expected a man to be nurturing and tough at the same time. Her father always told her that real men never put their hands on a woman. Leroy, on the other hand, was raised with both parents—in a dysfunctional home.

As Leroy continued, he shared that intimacy was lacking because what he wanted—aggressive sex—Octavia was unwilling and unable to give because of her excessive weight. That pushed him further away. He didn't understand how she let herself go. She stopped going to the hair salon. She stopped getting manicures and pedicures. She walked around the house in sweats all the time. She simply was no longer physically attractive to him.

Larry, however, knew the root of the "why".

He recalled the conversation he had with Octavia when she vaguely touched on her lack of desire because she knew of Leroy's affair. She was torn between trying to maintain her marriage and **not** lowering herself to a level of doing certain things in the bedroom for the sole purpose of keeping Leroy at home.

> *"For by grace you have been saved through faith. And this is not your own doing; it is the gift of God, not a result of works, so that no one may boast."*

Ephesians 2:8-9

The Roots of Infidelity Go DEEEEP

GOOD INTENTIONS AND DEMONS

With all of his good intentions, Larry's demons remained—and he was very aware of them. Being a minister gave him access to broken women who were attracted to prestige and power. He could almost be likened to a manager of a bar who was an alcoholic: He had too much access. It was virtually never-ending! Wednesday night bible study seemed like the perfect "meeting place", and he knew the temptation that flowed through his very being was all kinds of wrong.

He remembered that he had an appointment with Sharon coming up soon. Sharon was yet another member of the church who people viewed as a whore. She was always provocatively-dressed and known to be overly-friendly with the men. Larry wasn't naïve. He knew the potential was there that she had intentions that weren't appropriate for a married man. Trying his best to live an upright life before God and man, he needed to address at least whatever concerns she brought into the meeting.

Oh, the mind games we play with ourselves…

Sharon approached Larry a few weeks prior, asking if she could speak to him about some of the issues she was dealing with. She felt she couldn't talk to any of the women at the church because they were all judgmental. (Larry had already taken notice of how the women would look at her with obvious contempt.) He set the appointment with her, and the day had finally arrived.

Since bible study started at 7:00 p.m., he wanted to give her an hour and himself 30 minutes to shift gears after their meeting. On this particular day, the pastor was traveling, and Larry was responsible for the youth bible study. He needed to be prepared to deal with them. Thirty minutes should do it!

When she arrived and got settled, she asked if she could be very transparent with him. *"Of course!"* was his reply.

She began to speak, evasively at first…

"Every time I would see him, I would get this heightened sense of nervousness. My palms would sweat, and fear came over me. I still have nightmares at times. It's hard for me to get the visual of him

The Roots of Infidelity Go DEEEEP

putting his hand over my mouth as he forced himself inside of me. It happened when I was ten years old.

"My uncle, who was a pastor at the time, and his wife took me in because my dad took a job that had him traveling a lot. I learned in my teen years that he had also gotten heavily into drugs and was not in his right mind to come back for me. My aunt worked the graveyard shift at a hotel. Every time she would go to work, he would come into my room.

"I remember exiting the shower one day and, as I was drying off, he came into the bathroom and backed right out, shutting the door behind him. Not thinking anything of his sudden appearance because he seemed genuinely shocked that I was still in there, I continued drying off. When I put my bedclothes on and walked out, he said, "I'm sorry. I didn't realize you were still in there". All the while, he was holding my hand. That was the first time things seemed different.

As time went on, he went from holding my hand to coming into my bedroom more and more. On one hand, he spoiled me. I can't lie about that. I got everything I ever wanted. He made me feel like his own daughter at times, which felt good because my piss-poor father wasn't anywhere around. All I knew about 'dad' was that he was always working odd jobs to avoid paying child support. So, my uncle filled the role. There was nothing unusual to note at the time when he gave me fatherly hugs and kisses. I never thought things would turn into what has been haunting me all these years later.

"One night, he came into my room while I was asleep, grabbed my hand from underneath the cover, and had me stroking his penis. Startled out of my sleep, I pulled my hand back and looked at him in fear. He said, "It's okay, baby. I won't hurt you. I love you. Do you know that?" *I didn't know what to say or do, so I said nothing.* "Uncle won't hurt you," *he said and then left the room. I was terrified.*

"Not even a week later, not only did he force me to touch him; he ripped off my underwear, pinned me down, climbed on top of me, and raped me. It hurt so bad. He forced himself deeper and deeper inside of me. The pain was overwhelming. "If you say anything to anyone, I will hurt you, little girl," *he threatened.*

"From that moment, I have despised the ground men walk on. Every time I see my uncle, even in his old age, there is a feeling of hatred that overcomes me. The relationship between my aunt and me has changed as well. No one can tell me that she didn't know what was going on. Either she was too afraid to

The Roots of Infidelity Go DEEEEP

do anything, or she didn't care. I moved away as soon as I could and never looked back."

Larry had to cut things short. It was almost 6:30, and he was committed to that 30-minute break. He felt really bad for Sharon. Her story reminded him of the pain he's heard from countless others. He encouraged her not to keep her feelings bottled up and to try speaking with her uncle as a way to address the issue head-on. As well, that session gave Larry a different viewpoint as it related to how she was dealing with her demons. In some ways, he understood more than she would ever know. When she got up to walk out, she asked if they could meet again. Larry agreed.

They had two more sessions. It became apparent that not only did she want his listening ear; she also wanted to confess her attraction to him. *"You know, I want to thank you for listening to me. You don't have to do that. There is something else I want to share with you, but I'm unsure how you will take it."*

Larry had long ago noticed the tantalizing looks she gave him from time to time, hoping she would never address it.

"What is it?"

"I find you very attractive. I know it's inappropriate to mention, but I need you to know you are the talk amongst many women in the church."

"Thank you for the compliment," he replied. *"I hope it's all about God when they speak of me!"*

"Well, we say 'Thank you, God!' — but it's for selfish reasons." Larry had to chuckle at that one.

As she got up to leave, she bent over to retrieve her purse—displaying to him her bare naked rear end while asserting, *"Anything you need me to do, I will.* **ANYTHING***."*

The demon of lust inside of him couldn't let go of what he saw. He had to find a way to deal with it.

The Roots of Infidelity Go DEEEEP

THERE'S ALWAYS A HEFTY PRICE TO PAY

After Jules told her father that she knew about his affair, he responded by asking, *"What do you mean, baby girl?"* Bursting into tears, she told her dad **ALL** that she knew.

"Every time we went to church, I saw how she looked at you. I saw how many times she went into your office. She was known as the woman who would do anything to sleep with a man. You made her feel like she was number one while mom sat in the pews looking stupid. Everyone knew, dad! I stood by your office once and heard you going back and forth with her. The two of you argued as if you were a married couple. I heard you!"

"Baby girl…" he started to say. She cut him off.

*"Dad, stop. Do you have any idea what it was like for me as a child to hear those words coming from **YOUR** mouth?"*

She gave her father an almost verbatim replay of the moment she spent on the other side of the door listening to him…

"You know, I wish things could have been different, Sharon. There is so much that is happening right now, and it leads me right back to some of my original thoughts. For starters, all I said was 'Good morning! I hope you feel better.' *In my mind, it would have been selfish and shitty of me not to be concerned, given how I feel about you. Your comment about us both knowing it wasn't going to be easy took me back because it didn't have to be this way. It was a choice you made. I'm pissed because if you knew this wasn't what you wanted, you should have said something before we got this far. To cut me off cold turkey like you did, though? That hurts.*

"While I'm at it, I might as well address this: You seem confused about and unsure of who you want to be with. You tend to pick and choose which questions you answer. For example, when we were talking outside, I asked, 'Why do you continue to go back and forth with him?' *Your response was a blank look. I may be off about a lot of things, but I know what I see. I hate that you won't simply say what it is versus blowing up into a tantrum about it. Think about it: The issues you have with me are fixable. The problem here, however, is I'm not the one* **YOU** *want. There's this thing called "respect". You don't respect me or this relationship enough to cut him off. I don't expect you to act like you don't know him, but damn! Slow down*

the amount of time you spend communicating with him! Then, you bring him to this church as if he belongs. Well, he doesn't!

"These have been some trying times, to say the least. I truly believed you loved and cared for me, despite our situation. I really did. The joke is on me this time. God sure knew how to stick it to me! I would be lying if I said I was done with you. I would also be lying if I said I never wanted to see you again. In the end, I have to love me enough to accept what you're saying."

Jules' disappointment was obvious. *"Dad, I was shocked to hear you talk to another woman like that! It broke my heart. Up to that moment, I just knew for a fact the rumors about you weren't true. Then, the no-good tramp just stood there while you lectured her on your feelings for her. It was obvious the two of you had been having an affair behind mom's back for years.* That woman's response still flows through my head…"

"Typical Larry. Look, you don't contact me, and I won't contact you. We can wish each other the best and be done with this. You were never mine alone – as you claimed to be – let alone my pastor. You walked away from me with no explanation, like

*what we had meant nothing to you. So, stop blaming me. If it weren't for me, you wouldn't be looking to get divorced, and you wouldn't have cheated on me with Susan. So, not only did you cheat on your wife with **ME**, your no-good ass cheated on me with **ANOTHER** woman! And one who goes to the same damn church at that!*

"Now, I am left wondering how in the hell another woman in the same church gets what I worked so hard for. **I'M SUPPOSED TO BE THE FIRST LADY, LARRY!** *That's the promise you made me. You could care less about the damage you caused in my life because you are a selfish bastard. Every single time you needed me, I was right there. When I needed **YOU** the most, you bailed on me. You didn't think I deserved more than that?*

"Larry, the saddest part is you will never begin to understand the depth of pain you have caused my soul. You — of all people! The fact of the matter is as much as I wish I could, I don't have it in me to hurt you. Do you have any idea how many times I thought about telling the church?

"What we had was real to me. It's now something I have to live with. If you ever cared about me, you wouldn't have played with my heart and

emotions. I have to shoulder the responsibility for letting you get that one off. It's my struggle, not yours.

"Good luck to you both. I hope she's worth it. She got what I never had, but worked and even begged for from you. She gets to benefit from it all. I plan on working things out with my husband and put my family back together. You think I'm vindictive and that I'm out to hurt you. There are things I could tell you that would devastate you, but you will find them out in due time on your own. Just remember: I was the realest thing you have ever known. Maybe I should've been more like her. I dealt with all your crap and she won't. Perhaps that's the reason you chase her."

Larry had an answer for everything.

"Really? Look, hate me if you want. I don't hate you, though. I look at what has taken place between us and, unfortunately, there is still a lot of hurt to this day. The point is that I still deal with the repercussions of our actions. I've made a lot of poor decisions. It's time to move on and learn from it. I will always care about you. You can't do something for years and then act like it never happened.

"Yes, you were truly a friend when I didn't have anyone else. I will forever be grateful for that. We

shared a lot of personal things with one another. Of all people, you know me. I try hard not to be a person who hurts others. My 'getting over on people' days have been over for some time now. All I want is to get to a place where I don't have to worry about a thing…and I'm not there yet.

"I strayed far away from God. I ignored simple principles. I see the results of my actions as they manifested themselves in many ways, and I have to live with that. We have said and done a lot of hurtful things to one another. What was gained in the process? **NOTHING!** *As your friend who wants the best for you, I would never wish bad on you nor want you to be unhappy. You, too, have been through a lot. Don't let your hatred for me block your blessings.*

"From today forward, I wish you all the best. There is no need for hostile communication. Again, I can't throw away years of our being together as if they didn't exist. You were my friend, for goodness sake! I hope that one day, we can be friends again, as I believe you are a good friend to many people. I know you mean well for everyone you come across. It's apparent, though, that today is not a day when we can communicate on a friendly level."

The Roots of Infidelity Go DEEEEP

Jules paused to acknowledge the change in atmosphere in the room before she admonished her father.

*"And to think dad: You had not one, but **two** affairs! To have the tramp walking around like she owned the place was ridiculous to me. Come to find out; she's married, too? How sick and twisted could that be? You dare to ask me why I didn't come to church? All of you are the same! I'll **never** marry a man who's involved in the church!*

"When you and mom divorced, I carried that burden of knowing what you did for many years. I watched as mom fell apart. I know, I know: Give it to God, right? Where was your God when my mom cried every night? Where was your God when you were sleeping with other women in the church? Look how long it took for mom to come back around to being herself. Your actions caused her to become bitter and unpleasant with everyone. I don't think I can ever forgive you for doing what you did to my mom."

> *"Put on the full armor of God, so that you can take your stand against the devil's schemes."*

Ephesians 6:11

The Roots of Infidelity Go DEEEEP

WHEN YOU'VE DONE ALL TO STAND...

Having grown up in the church, Jules went through many years of inner turmoil. There were countless times she was depressed with no one to talk to. For years, she stood all alone.

In a moment of solace, while being trapped inside of her own thoughts, she talked aloud to herself to give voice to her reality...

"I feel like I'm the Twilight Zone. I'm speaking, but no one seems to understand. I'm screaming, and no one hears me. I'm drowning, while people are walking by. I feel like I just want to run away.

"I can't believe my mom knew what was going on and chose to stay. My dad made us all look like fools. I just want to start all over in a new place. However, I'm reminded that you reap what you sow and that God is not to be mocked. Dad's day of reckoning must come because God cannot and does not lie.

"It's so hard to hold on. Everyone in the church pretended they were happy, yet they secretly desired other things...and people. As for me, I had so many years to get right, but I kept playing around and forcing God to step in and deal with me. I'm faced with

the reality that the happiness I seek will always allude me. While I cannot live in the past, my past choices continue to dictate my present.

"Why am I here, faced to deal with this alone? I hope to get to a place where I will one day understand. Meanwhile, I drown in a sea of my horrid thoughts daily. I'm convinced everything is a lie and everyone is a liar."

LOYAL TO 'SELF' ONLY

Jules' difficulties in life were compounded when her mom died before Jules had the opportunity to share her hurts. Jules became a wreck. What took her over the edge was learning how bad things really were between her parents via a letter she found. Her mom had written the letter to her dad but never mailed it. It read:

"I was a horrible person to be married to. I was embarrassed by you. I put you down. I didn't make you feel valued. Nothing you ever did was good enough. I was unbelievably selfish and cared only about my own happiness. I needed you to fill the vacant holes in my life, and you needed me to make up for your childhood. We were more in love with the idea of love than love itself.

"I was ashamed of my choices and the life I had. I feel my friends all made better choices and were living what I perceived were better lives. When you and I met, my first impression was that you were some lame man, never suspecting you would come to lead a church. I was angry and bitter. You were the perfect victim for my wrath because you kept coming back for more. You never could be alone…

"You have always had the need to be accepted. The approval of others is so important to you, even now. You have never been sure of yourself, which is why you've never been able to lead. You need someone to follow, which is why you steal facets of others' lives and make them your own.

"In all honesty, we couldn't love each other because we didn't love ourselves. I didn't think I was worthy of love because I hadn't accomplished all the things I felt were important. You saw me as a challenge more than you ever loved me. Although we were young, stupid, and selfish, we stepped into God's arena by getting married. That set us on a path of destruction—one that neither of us could have ever imagined. There were so many opportunities for us to get it right, but neither of us would bend. We would make little adjustments at best, only to return to our old ways. That was until God had had enough. He stepped in and exposed your true identity. He used your true identity to expose all my lies. In response, you destroyed my pride by publicly embarrassing and forcing me to deal with me. No longer did I do things my way. No longer did I adjust my life to suit my needs. I submitted fully to God's will.

*"I have cried more in the past two years than I have in my entire life. Losing my parents **AND** you*

The Roots of Infidelity Go DEEEEP

have been ordeals that put me in a dark place. I see now that I left God no other choice.

"Regardless of how I felt, I was wrong to treat you like I did. You didn't deserve that. I didn't know how to love. I didn't realize I had a role to fill in giving love; not just receiving it. I feared rejection if you didn't respond the way I wanted you to when I expressed myself. Eventually, you got tired of trying. Eight years is a long time to try to reach a person's heart without success. When I finally surrendered and realized what love was, you had already begun to rebel. There was nothing left to repair.

"Let me say this: You were not crazy. I apologize for making you feel that you were. I did lay next to you while wishing I was somewhere else. I intentionally hurt, belittled, and disrespected you at times. I was completely outside of God's will, and you were the recipient of my hurts. For that, I'm sorry. If I ever made you feel like I felt when we first split up, I apologize for that as well. Made to feel not good enough; I'm sorry. Made to feel replaceable; I'm sorry. So easily discarded like you never mattered; I'm sorry. You tried to get back at me. You believed (and still believe) that you could've shown me better than you could've told me. All you did was hurt yourself and strayed farther away from God. No one can escape

judgment. I know I certainly didn't. That made me a better person, which is why I can say what I'm about to say:

"Larry, you are lost. You have no direction because God does not guide your life. We think we can just live our lives free of His laws. We are wrong! Ecclesiastes 8:11 states, "Because sentence against an evil work is not executed speedily. Therefore the heart of the sons of men is fully set in them to do evil." *Basically, because God doesn't deal with our sins right away, we keep doing them, not realizing mercy is being extended towards us to get ourselves right before He has to step in. Sin blinds us to reality. I have paid for my noncompliance to God's commandments and my abuse of you. I have no doubt the time will come when you will have to answer for yours, too.*

"I want you to remember how you felt as a child when James wasn't there, how unimportant you felt. You swore you would never do that to Jules. Well, although you were there, you still left her. You dished out the same pain that your family dished out to you. You held in being molested for many years. You never addressed it, Larry. What did you do? You swept it under the rugs as if it never happened. You allowed it to consume your whole life. It altered the way you saw

The Roots of Infidelity Go DEEEEP

yourself. All the promises made to her meant nothing anymore. All the talks about how men don't lie went out the door. Wanting to marry a man just like her daddy went out the door. I can always believe in daddy went out the door. She is lost, Larry! And I can't reach her.

"I want you to understand that this is bigger than an attitude or not responding to any of your calls over the years. I'm talking about what cannot be seen with the natural eye. Imagine how your daughter – at 16 years old – was on detective websites trying to learn how to know if her father was having an affair. Imagine how little Kevin (with tears in his eyes) had to be the one to tell me about the text messages his sister had been reading between you and Sharon, only because she couldn't bear to tell me herself. I want you to imagine how she had to be excused from class because the teacher was reading a story with a character named 'Sharon' and she started to cry. Imagine how just four months ago, she was so emotional while talking about her feelings, we had to end our conversation.

"She wants to come live with you so she can see you more because she desperately misses you. I am guilty of penalizing her for desiring what is natural. It is natural for children to want their parents to be together. Every day, we are teaching them that God's

way is abnormal and that they can create a new normal.

*"I shared with my friend a conversation I had with your daughter, and that 40-year-old woman began to cry as she remembered how she felt after her parents' divorce. I want you to understand what we have done and how we have incurred the wrath of God because of what we have done to our daughter. We have taught her that there is an alternative life by giving her the option to determine what is best for her outside of God's commandments. I'm in the best place of my life right now, but how can I rejoice when my child is not? You were so busy trying **NOT** to be fake, that you forgot to be a parent. You forgot to protect her. Where was your concern when you repeatedly broke my heart? Now you want what you were unwilling to give?*

"I love you. I forgive you and Sharon, but you will feel the pain of your choices. God does not change. His commands are to be obeyed. He will mix His mercy with the pain, but you will still feel the sting so that you will not be so quick to sin against Him again.

"I don't know what your belief system is in this moment, Larry. I don't know what you know about God or how you want to live the rest of your life. Hell,

The Roots of Infidelity Go DEEEEP

do you even believe what you've preached to all those people who follow you and not God? One thing I know: God will not be mocked. Children are precious in His sight, and when we cause them pain or cause them to question Him and His ways, God will act against us. What we did was wrong. If we think we will walk away Scott-free, we are in for a rude awakening.

"You got dressed and toted a Bible every Sunday. Then, you committed adultery in the sight of God. He watched you. Believe that. You taught your daughter that a man's word means nothing. You gave Satan an opportunity to come in and use it against her. God watched. You took your covering away from your daughter, so now she looks to other men for advice instead of you. God watched.

"There is no peace, saith the Lord, unto the wicked" (Isaiah 48:22).

"This isn't a plea for reconciliation; this is a reality check — a call to righteousness and sounding of the alarm. I don't know who has your ear or who you seek for wisdom, but if they haven't shared this with you, you can stop wondering how and just repair your relationship with her. Understand that the real cause of your unrest is because they haven't shared much of anything with you. God's Word is true,

whether we believe it or not. The point of repentance is to stop doing wrong. We can't apologize and continue in sin. The liar stops lying. The thief no longer steals. The fornicator no longer fornicates."

"Now we know that God heareth not sinners: but if any man be a worshipper of God, and doeth His will, him He heareth" (John 9:31).

"But fornication, and all uncleanness, or covetousness, let it not be once named among you, as becometh saints; neither filthiness, nor foolish talking, nor jesting, which are not convenient: but rather giving of thanks. For this ye know, that no whoremonger, nor unclean person, nor covetous man, who is an idolater, hath any inheritance in the kingdom of Christ and of God" (Ephesians 5:3-5).

"There is a way which seemeth right unto a man, but the end thereof are the ways of death" (Proverbs 14:12).

"Can a man take fire in his bosom, and his clothes not be burned? Can one go upon coals, and his feet not be burned? So he that goeth into his neighbor's wife; whosoever toucheth her shall not be innocent. Men do not despise a thief if he steals to satisfy his soul when he is hungry; but if he be found, he shall restore

sevenfold; he shall give all the substance of his house. But whoso committeth adultery with a woman lacketh understanding: he that doeth it destroyeth his own soul" (Proverbs 6:27-32).

"Know ye not, brethren, (for I speak to them that know the law), how that the law hath dominion over a man as long as he liveth? For the woman which hath an husband is bound by the law to her husband so long as he liveth; but if the husband be dead, she is loosed from the law of her husband. So then if, while her husband liveth, she be married to another man, she shall be called an adulteress: but if her husband be dead, she is free from the law; so that she is no adulteress, though she be married to another" (Romans 7:1-3).

"And unto the married I command, yet not I, but the Lord: Let not the wife depart from her husband; but if she depart, let her remain unmarried, or be reconciled to her husband: and let not the husband put away his wife" (1 Corinthians 7:10-11).

"And hereby we do know that we know him if we keep his commandments. He that saith, I know Him and keepeth not His commandments, is a liar, and the truth is not in him. But whoso keepeth His Word in him verily is the love of God perfected: hereby, we know

that we are in Him. He that saith he abideth in Him ought himself also so to walk, even as He walked" (1 John 2:3-6).

"Blessed are they that do His commandments that they may have a right to the Tree of Life, and may enter in through the gates into the city. For without are dogs, and sorcerers, and whoremongers, and murderers, and idolaters, and whosoever loveth and maketh a lie" (Revelation 22:14-15).

"Larry, I encourage you: Embrace those passages, my love. Get back in God's face and get the direction you so desperately need but have strayed from. Be the man God created you to be – for yourself and your child."

Signed,

Your Wife

Jules is mentally scarred. What awaits Pat?

The Roots of Infidelity Go DEEEEP

LET YOUR LIFE SPEAK YOUR WORTH

At this point, Pat is flirting with greed—and he doesn't even see it! He has no clue what awaits him as it relates to Jules. She may be cute and have pretty eyes, but she is a savage inside. Like most people, he couldn't see beyond the surface.

~~~~~~~~~~

Our greed is fed by our eyes and what we think we want. Greed (also known as avarice, cupidity, or covetousness) is a lot like lust and gluttony. It is a sin of desire. However, greed is applied to an artificial, rapacious desire and pursuit of material possessions. Wanting everything or, better yet, never having enough can and will cost you more than you bargained for.

Greed is something that has crippled many people for years. Sure, on the surface, we can easily toss around reasons for people's greed or identify with one's need for wanting more. In my opinion, greed goes far deeper than what's on the surface. Our sense of being is often attached to needing certain things, and when don't have them, we seek 'it' in the oddest places.

For example, from a rich person's perspective, money doesn't buy them happiness, but it sure can get him or her a good time where happiness resides. Putting it plainly: Many are lonely. Now, that's not to say they don't have the means to have someone laying next to them at night, but when they tire of that company, they replace them with someone new and fresh. Money can't and never will buy a sense of peace…that sense of knowing when you wake up in the morning, you have that person who makes you want to wake up in their arms every day. That feeling is almost indescribable to me.

Like most people, we may desire a particular 'thing'. When we get it, we realize we want something else. Before you know it, the cycle of wanting more creeps into our lives and then **BOOM**! We are caught up. Throughout our lives, we have all been in a state of "want" at one time or another — and that is totally okay! Why *NOT* want more, right?

The Roots of Infidelity Go DEEEEP

It's funny how that concept dates back to the days of man wanting more than one wife. 'Concubine' would have never been a word we would know if it wasn't something that was done (legally) before this day and age. Greed can only be relevant when something or someone allows the want to be fulfilled. Have you ever considered the actual concubine or mistress? Why would one want to be second best? People rarely take a look into their mental state until it's too late. We find it easier to look at the one who openly does wrong, while rarely admonishing those who accept it.

Think of it like this: It's no different than standing in a room full of people talking about someone. Isn't entertaining the conversation just as bad? Let me laugh for a moment at your utter disagreement… I insist, however: When you think about it, why do we measure the wrongdoing of a person's actions if the wrong is defined in different versions or by different scales? By definition, right is right…and wrong is wrong.

Moving along…

Greed will change your life in so many ways. Don't be fooled by contentment. Some confuse contentment with complacency or settling. They are quite different. In my humble opinion, contentment and peace walk the same line.

Some of us have a hard time trying to figure out why people do half the things they do, especially cheating. Some people have gone as far as to research the topic. Others have formulated a strong opinion on why people step outside of their relationships. The fact is that there are many variations on the 'why' and not enough questions asked about the 'what'. For me, the 'what' outweighs the 'why', as the 'why' is derived from the 'what'. You wouldn't ask, *"Why does a car stall?"*; rather, you would ask, *"What made the car stall?"*

While in a relationship, if we asked what made you cheat, we will more than likely get to the root of the issue. Once we get to the root, we can then decide whether or not we are willing to deal with the process. For starters, the 'what' can be from having a problem that goes unaddressed mentally or perhaps stemming from a feeling of

The Roots of Infidelity Go DEEEEP

needing more. In my personal experience, life is what was lacking. I have heard things such as, *"I am not happy,"* which is probably the **broadest** answer anyone can give. Happiness evolves out of things happening, so, again, it goes back to the 'what'. **WHAT** makes you unhappy? If we keep asking 'what', I am confident we can get to the deepest root — which, for men and women, can be different *OR* the same. *"**WHAT** made me lie to my significant other?"* I did not **have** to lie. I **chose** to lie because I want to keep my current situation intact.

Trying to pinpoint a generic reason will have you losing sleep. To be perfectly honest, unless you see everything, hear everything, or participate in everything, you will never know every detail about his or her affairs. Surface issues are that of a person experiencing a bad tragedy in which they excuse their wrong when, in fact, the bad experience was nothing more than a bridge they used to cross over, rather than crossing over alone and I the right frame of mind.

What I find worse than being cheated on is all the other things that come with it: the lies, the mind games, the disrespectfulness. There is nothing worse than being made a fool of, especially when everyone knows but you — because now, what could have been just between the two of you is has ballooned into a bigger issue. Cheaters don't see that bigger picture. All they see is themselves getting a temporary high while trying to cover each track as they go. We are so far removed from the days of people being honest. So many have lived a lie to the point that they cannot recognize the truth. What is there to be gained by living a lie? Perhaps they think acceptance comes with living a lie. Our actions are that of wanting and needing validation, but how can anyone validate you better than yourself? You shouldn't need anyone to tell you your worth. Instead, your life and actions should speak your worth to the point that you attract those who are worthy to be in your presence.

We bring our deep-rooted problems into relationships without realizing that when we bring a suitcase full of problems to anything, most aren't eager to help us unpack. After all, they didn't put the baggage in there!

There is nothing anyone can do to stop another person from doing what his or her heart

The Roots of Infidelity Go DEEEEP

and mind are set on doing. We are, however, accustomed to doing what the masses do. We go with the wave that is currently moving instead of finding our own wave to ride. Here again is another example of us as people wanting to be "in the know". Have you ever wondered why so few solid relationships exist? Well, have you ever made pudding out of two rocks? The same applies to taking two stubborn people, expecting them to make a change. Unless they are both willing to be crushed down to a mental place of redemption and renewal, change will never happen!

Do yourself a favor and always remember: What is meant for **YOU** will be *JUST* for you.

> "But I tell you that anyone who looks at a woman lustfully has already committed adultery with her in his heart."

Matthew 5:28

The Roots of Infidelity Go DEEEEP

THE BODY SPEAKS

Interestingly enough, another aspect that many miss the mark on is sloth. In laymen's terms, sloth is simply defined as being too damn lazy. So many of us do not take heed to this characteristic, and, in some cases, don't see the connection between being lazy and not meeting the needs of a relationship.

If the person you are with told you flat out that you are boring, chances are likely you will become defensive and miss the overall point he or she was trying to make. From personal experience, the most talked about form of laziness comes when one complains about their sex life (or lack thereof). One of the parties can't wrap their mind around putting in the work in the bedroom for whatever the reason. The truth is (from my male perspective) that some of you women are beyond lazy in bed. All you want is someone to take care of you and make it all about you. It takes **TWO** people to 'make it happen'. Then, you want to be all up in your feelings when you catch him watching porn or constantly wanting to go with the fellas to the strip club. Hell, if you can't [won't?] move in the bed, at least let him watch someone else move, right? Of course, that's not the correct approach; however, in all fairness, who wants to lay with someone who is like a log sitting in water? **NO ONE!** The challenge in this situation is knowing how to address the issue without creating another one. The hope is that one can share what they are lacking and the other receives the remark from a place of wanting to work things through.

Now, it goes both ways, men. A woman wants a man who will get up in the morning, go to work, come home, and make it all about her. When it's time to make love, she wants you to put it on her—just like that first time. A woman has a desire to be turned on by a male who calls himself a man. Mentally, all of this goes deep; and for that reason, I believe that's why many haven't tapped into the real issues.

To the ladies: Do you think men don't notice when things are 'off' with you? Let's take, for example, he loses his job. What was once an every day or every other day intimacy level turned into something of an obligation because you—as the woman—are left feeling like you now have to hold it down. Your body indirectly responds in a way that makes it hard for you to be around. You don't feel like being sexy any longer because your mind is focused on work, work, work. God forbid you come home and see him just sitting there. The first thing that would come to mind is, *"What in the hell did he do all day?"* You never stop to think that looking for a job is a job in itself! What you didn't see was him slaving at the computer all day, sending out resumes left and right. He needed a moment before he went to task again, yet all you see is him "relaxing". That is the best-case-scenario in that instance. The opposite side of the coin is that he spent all day playing video games and sipping beers. I advise you to not jump to conclusions and simply **ASK**: *"How did the job search go today?"* — and **THEN** respond accordingly. Leave the assumptions at the door.

Of course, there are so many scenarios that can be presented here; however, at no point should either of you neglect the other's needs. Even if you find yourself unable to meet the need, most people want (at minimum) acknowledgment of what they **HAVE** done. Let them know if they are doing something right. Express that while you are doing all you can, you may have to adjust a few things to provide exactly what the other needs.

Should laziness drive people to cheat? Absolutely not! But it sure as hell doesn't help the situation, either.

What's unfortunate is that when infidelity creeps into a relationship, the trust is so hard to repair. The smallest things turn into larger issues. The crazy part is that the one who cheats is probably more on guard than the one who was cheated on! Think about **THAT**!

The Roots of Infidelity Go DEEEEP

TEMPTATIONS AND PLEAS

Time marched on. Brandy and Pat continue to try and work through what seems like a mountain of issues that lay dormant under the surface. Brandy had already made up in her mind that trusting him would be a challenge, as she sure wasn't going to put up with him hitting her! Those thoughts drove her crazy!

For Pat, the bigger issue was dealing with the fact that Brandy cheated. This constantly played on his mind, which would lead him to 'think' about his old ways. Turning back to those ways wasn't the real problem, however; it was the constant presence of temptation. Why now? Why, after Brandy is in his life? Why, after they try to work things out? **Why? Why? Why?**

Pat's temptation...

One particular instance when Pat was faced with temptation was when Megan reached out to him. No big deal, right? After all, when they were in high school, they dated for a while. The only precious memories that remained were those of late-night conversations and her buying him a sweater for his birthday.

They met when they both worked at the mall. When he walked into Champs, she was standing there helping a customer. He wanted to be **HER** next customer. Sure, someone else could have helped him, but there was something about the way she stood. She had the look and confidence of a model. In his young mind, Pat immediately knew he wanted to be with her — and he achieved the mark! They dated for a while as teens and then, as time went on, they lost contact over the years.

Now, as adults, she reached out to him via social media. One day, lost in his feelings of being alone, a Friend Request notification popped up on his Facebook page. Nothing unusual there. After all, that was his way of catching up with old friends. When he clicked the notification, it was Megan. Her profile picture was of her sitting by the water, looking out into the ocean as if she was looking for someone or something. His heart began racing. He couldn't believe that after all that time, she still looked as beautiful as the young girl he first met. He immediately accepted the request and messaged her. *"Hey, stranger!"* She quickly replied. *"Stranger is right! How have you been?"*

The Roots of Infidelity Go DEEEEP

It was around 10:00 p.m. that particular night when the exchange began. Brandy had been asleep for some time now, as was routine. Pat would wind down after a long day at work by eating and watching *Power*.

Megan and Pat chatted back and forth via Facebook, reminiscing and catching up. When 11:30 came, neither of them were ready to end the conversation; however, as mind games go, he had to make sure he didn't give off the wrong impression, especially since she knew he was married. He typed, *"Well, let me let you go. I don't want to keep you up too late"*.

"I'm fine, but I don't want to keep you away from your family, so I will let **YOU** *go."*

"Do you think we could…? Never mind", he replied.

The cat-and-mouse game with the subtle flirting began. Knowing he was playing a dangerous game, he chose to keep it 100 and tell her he needed to end the chat, as it wouldn't end well. The next morning, Pat told Brandy about his conversation with Megan out of respect for her, but that opened a door that would never close. The trust was broken.

As time went on, Pat found himself going out alone…often. Brandy wasn't having it and chose not to accept it for the innocence that it was. He pleaded his case:

"I have been trying to find the words to tell you. I am having a hard time articulating it in a way that wouldn't sound mean or inconsiderate. I really am remorseful. I find it interesting that something so meaningless to me is what breaks the camel's back for you. The situation with Sarah was intentional and a reaction to how I used to deal with situations. This, on the other hand, has nothing to do with ill-intent or trying to get back at you.

"I have turned into the person I never wanted to be. I ask myself all that time why I accept certain things and why I operate in certain ways. All I know is I have and continue to operate out of my pain, struggling with how to be a man and what I feel a man is. I have allowed people and things to control my life. I have done so much for so many people, all the while neglecting me. In turn, I neglected those things that were important.

The Roots of Infidelity Go DEEEEP

"Now, I am not in a relationship with anyone else. I don't have room in my life and, most importantly, I wouldn't bring in a relationship with you still being in my life. Despite everything else, I cannot and will not move on with someone else with you in my life. It just couldn't happen. None of what has taken place has been about your looks, your sense of being, nor anything familiar. It has been about me and how I respond to certain things.

"It's like that for a lot of people. If I don't make you feel pretty and another man tells you that you are, you will receive it. In this case, when I feel like less than a man or not good enough for you, I react. Lately, it's been about just disconnecting.

"I wanted to hang out because I felt it would have been a way for me to do what I wanted and not what others wanted. I didn't tell you because I didn't want to tell you. You were already going through, and my telling you would have introduced a trust issue. I would have stayed home because you wanted me to and not because I wanted to. I do so much based upon what you feel. I don't feel I have the opportunity to be a man. I feel like I have to ask permission for everything, and I simply don't like it. So, I did what I wanted to do with no ill-intent involved. I had a few drinks, and that was

it. I did not have sex with anyone; neither did I set out to hurt you.

"All in all, I could be that guy who checks in with my whereabouts all the time, but I feel I've done that my entire life. I want to share things with you because I want to; not out of obligation. Even in a marriage, people do things out of obligation. That stops people from being true to themselves.

"Brandy, you are in my life for a reason. It's because I love and care about you. I want us to work, in spite of all the cheating that has taken place. My commitment to you is my choice. You make me feel like I have you in a prison, as you clearly desire to be with someone else whom, as you say, you can trust. You were saying those things before I ever gave you a reason not to trust me. Your constant threats about leaving me for another man makes me want to run. I don't understand why women think threatening a man with the presence of another man is productive. As a man, I am telling you that **NO MAN** *wants to be threatened with another man.*

"I needed an outlet, Brandy. I wasn't trying to hurt you. Lately, that outlet has been drinking. My life is consumed with you and my thoughts about you. I love you so much!"

The Roots of Infidelity Go DEEEEP

Brandy felt her rage softening, but she couldn't let Pat think he was going to get off the hook **THAT** easily.

"Watch over your heart with all diligence, for from it flow the springs of life."

Proverbs 4:23

The Roots of Infidelity Go DEEEEP

HELP IS ONE THOUGHT AWAY

Understanding the true depths of the damage infidelity causes should steer people off of that path, correct? Someone once shared with me the following words of wisdom:

"If you think you can, you will.
If you think you can't, you won't!"

After hearing those words, I recall how drastically I changed the things I did. I have always felt like I can achieve anything; however, I also knew there were certain things I wouldn't *ALLOW* myself to do because I was afraid to step out on a limb and just **DO** them.

We all have heard the words *"I pledge allegiance to the flag of the United States of America…"* at some point or another in our lives. As a child, I remember having to recite them day in and day out while in school. Not once did I question why. As I grew older and started to take interest in asking the 'Why?' question, I found myself becoming more in touch with my inquisitive mind. I came to believe that many people do things without question and, as a result, become part of the majority.

The minority is the group of people who refuse to accept life as "normal".

Throughout the years, I have faced many difficult challenges in both my personal life and in relationships. As I reflect on those times, there were some instances when, given the opportunity, I would have made a different choice. Working through conflicts can be tough at times, especially in relationships. However, I am grateful for those opportunities, as they became bridges I once crossed. Crossing over is a voyage. Growth is a process.

As I continue on my journey, I constantly seek ways to improve areas where I am weak. In doing so, I also try to help anyone and everyone I can along the way…one relationship at a time.

FRACTURED; NOT QUITE BROKEN

As you go through life, never allow anyone to tell you what you can't do. In the same breath, never let anyone come in between your relationship. Your relationship can be a successful one. Having a successful relationship should be something both of you want. There's no way to know in advance the direction it's heading, but surely, you have a vision of what the result will be. Through difficulties and roadblocks, the view of success may become slightly skewed. Be mindful that you will always face a challenge along the way. You will not always arrive exactly where you want to be. Keep moving, though!

All your life, you may have been battling something—a demon that only you and God know exists. As an adult, you find yourself still battling that 'thing', and you both look and feel worn down and out. It's a natural feeling. Living in that space for a moment is okay. The time is **NOW** when you must trust that God will lead you to exactly where you *NEED* to be.

So many people have trust issues, and the legitimacy of them stems from past issues and reminders of them. We have developed a sense of protecting our feelings that comes across as insecurity when, in fact, many are not insecure with themselves but rather the fractured — **NOT BROKEN** — relationship. When you hear people say that a relationship (especially marriage) is work, it truly is. That's not to be confused with a typical day job. They are referring to the effort to be the best at making it last. Too many times, people miss that point. With their tunnel-vision, they only see what they want to see. The best companion considers the other without question. It's not about being in control or submitting to another; it's about having an equal amount of responsibility.

Note the following: Everyone isn't against you. Just because one door closed doesn't mean every door will close. God will **ALWAYS** do things in **HIS** timing; not ours. To be in a state of knowing means you can use that time to allow God to speak to you. Stop holding on to the negative aspects of this world. Start looking at the positives — even if it's only one. Rest assured that God still has His hands on you. How do I know?

The Roots of Infidelity Go DEEEEP

Because He woke you up and gave you another chance! Stop beating yourself up and start seeking **JOY**!

"I urge you, brothers and sisters, to watch out for those who cause divisions and put obstacles in your way that are contrary to the teaching you have learned. Keep away from them."

Romans 16:17

The Roots of Infidelity Go DEEEEP

THE SICK MERRY-GO-ROUND

Throughout his years, Joseph has encountered a lot of people, all walking in different places in life; family, friends, associates, and even distant relatives. Each had their own stories about life's mountains they had to climb.

There were many times he found himself wondering why there is so much of the same thing going on with everyone he came into contact with. If they weren't the one cheating, they were being cheated on. If they weren't abused as a child, they were being abused mentally, verbally, or physically as an adult. They were doing things that could cost them their very lives! Rarely did a diamond in the rough show up. The cycle of life seemed to have the vast majority on the sick merry-go-round.

To Joseph, it appeared that everyone was simply 'making it' — one day at a time. Either they were getting their hustle on or finding a way to hustle someone else. The "eat or get eaten" attitude takes over. The most interesting aspect of it all is that as a people, he realized they are quick to find the problem in others while bypassing the truth: They are their own problem! Wouldn't it be an awesome shift if the world would start to look within first? *"That's too much like 'right',"* he mused.

Joseph had a cousin he was very close with by the name of Ken. Ken was very interesting. He was 'that guy' who always wanted to make everyone laugh through their pain. He made everything into a joke, even when the joke was on him. Like many others, he had his fair share of undealt-with issues.

Ken had the weight of the world on his shoulders, yet no one knew it. Being a friend to both Joseph and Pat, he was no stranger to always having to deal with a bad hand. His view of life appeared to change with each challenge he faced. For some, challenges would be seen as another way of testing one's strength. For Ken, he was beyond the idea of being tested by God. Instead, he had the mentality that everything was bad until it was proven to be good. He lived his life anticipating things going wrong. As it related to his love life, he refused to give any woman he was with a fair chance. Having been exposed to sex at a very young age and witnessing some sick behaviors by adults, Ken's view had always been warped.

Ken remembered when...

It was during the summer of 1996; a time when the world as he knew it was a bit more at ease and the approach of the end of an era in which the hunt became more of a thrill than the actual kill was on the horizon. Speaking in laymen's terms, it was when chasing the fine girls was far better than actually sleeping with them.

One afternoon, my grandparents went for their weekly trip to the store. I knew that this would be the day I would lose my virginity. No longer playing house with my cousins and friends, I was ready to become a man. Even though playing house was fun back then (as we rubbed against each other as if we knew what we were doing), what I imagined for my first time was nothing like that. Imitating what I saw on TV, I envisioned how I would hold her. What was it about playing house that kept me looking forward to the weekends when she would come over? As it turned out, time for playing house was over.

Like clockwork, after my grandparents left, I couldn't wait for my next-door neighbor, Darlene, to come over. The only problem we had was getting rid of her little brother, Justin. What were we supposed to do with him while we did what we had to do? After all, it's not like we had all day. We needed to get to the business of doing "it" quickly! Not willing to wait a second longer, I ran next door to get her. Justin answered the door.

"Hi, Ken! Do you want to go play basketball in the backyard?"

Quick on my feet, I replied, "I'll be right there. How about your practice your layups while I run to the store to grab us two sodas?"

Justin excitedly ran out the back door and, just as I knew he would, started working on his layups. I told him I would be back in 20 minutes and not to stop practicing until I returned. Big Momma had two sodas in the refrigerator, so I was covered there. Off to my house, Darlene and I went.

Darlene was known around the neighborhood as having sex a 'time or two'. We knew she dated Donald, the known drug dealer in the hood. For me, I didn't care if she dated Donald or Ronald McDonald; all I wanted at the ripe age of 14 was to finally get what everyone else was talking about – a piece of the pie!

The Roots of Infidelity Go DEEEEP

My heart was racing, and I was a nervous wreck. She knew she was about to be my first. She had a dress on with no panties underneath. I couldn't wait! As she laid on her back in the bed, I had to ask for her help as I crawled on top of her. "Put it in for me," *I said in my young, seductive, Similac-smelling-breath voice. She chuckled, grabbed a hold of my penis, and expertly guided me inside of her. Off to the races, I went…until the sensation of having to pee suddenly overcame me.*

Not able to shake the feeling, I told her, "Wait. I really have to pee". *Reflecting back, the 'knowing' grin on her face was all too telling. It said,* "Ummhmm. **THAT** is **not** what you're feeling!" *Somehow, I missed the significance of that look.*

I stood over the toilet trying my hardest to pee, but nothing came out. I flushed the toilet anyway and returned to Darlene. I was still rock-hard aroused and got back into position – just as Justin yelled, **"OOOOO! I'M TELLING MAMA!"** *He was standing there looking at me laying on top of his sister.*

I jumped out of bed and begged him not to tell. I tried to bribe him by telling him I would give him anything he wanted. Darlene, looking nervous, said something to Justin that would change my view of her forever.

> "I will let you do it, too,
> if you don't say anything."

Stunned by those words and not wanting to get in trouble, I stood there looking back and forth between the two. Justin rushed past me while yanking down his pants. He jumped on top of her and began pounding away. It was obvious this was nothing new for them and likely something they did in their spare time. I stood there in awe as I watched Darlene allow her little brother to have sex with her for all of two minutes. Not knowing what to say or do, I finally managed to drum up the words, "My grandparents will be home soon." *That prompted them to get up hurriedly and leave my house.*

Feeling somewhat relieved to have finally lost my virginity, I was somewhat taken aback by what I just witnessed. Playing house with cousins and friends was one thing, but sex among siblings? That altered my way of thinking, yet it didn't tarnish my desire to want that feeling again.

Monday came fast, and school was the place to be. For me, that was the day I could walk a little

The Roots of Infidelity Go DEEEEP

smoother with my friends who didn't think I would get it done. The change in my swagger must have been obvious. "So, are you still a virgin?" *Tony asked.* "Do I look like one?" *I replied with confidence.*

Having the feeling of being "in" was something I could check off my internal list of things I was tired of people asking about. For me, it was deeper than losing my virginity. It was now about knowing there was nothing wrong with me.

I fought with a demon for a long time and finally felt I had won the battle. It felt good to affirm I was attracted to only women. I still couldn't understand how a man – a "Godly" man – would ever do what he did to me.

> *"But because of the temptation to sexual immorality, each man should have his own wife and each woman her own husband."*

1 Corinthians 7:2

HE VIOLATED ME—I'M A BOY!

Ken still had nightmares. Each time, he was awakened by the sight of that man's face in his dreams. He was too afraid to say anything out of fear of being laughed at. Just the mere thought of going back to that same church where 'he' was every week made Ken cringe. The church had a weekend camping event scheduled for just the boys. He was excited about the opportunity to hang with his friends and do all the cool stuff that goes along with camping out.

Never in a million years did he think what happened to him would take place while on that trip.

Ken reflects back on that dreadful day…

I remember standing by the water, fishing pole in hand. Pastor Mike came over and helped me with the stuck reel. Having had experience with fishing (thanks to my grandfather), I thought I could fix the problem. It turned out, there was a kink in the line due to rust on the reel.

"Ken, let me help you fix that," Pastor Mike said. I handed him the rod and reel and watched as he

expertly repaired the reel. When he was done, he said, "I want to try fishing in the dark. Do you want to come with me?" *I thought Pastor Mike was the coolest and happily agreed. I felt honored that he asked **ME** to join him and not any other camper, and looked forward to the nighttime adventure!*

When nightfall came, I ran out of the camp and headed for the water. Walking with his flashlight, Pastor Mike approached and said, "Great night for fishing! I hope you're ready to catch some GOOD fish!"

We cast our lines and waited for a bite. I felt a slight tug on my line. "I got one! I got one!" *I happily exclaimed. Together, we both grabbed the line and started to reel in what felt like a big catch. Struggling to reel it in, Pastor Mike positioned himself behind me. He grabbed the rod and was uncomfortably close to me. Unaware of what was about to take place, I tried to reposition myself so that he could take over the duties of pulling in the fish single-handedly. Clearly, that wasn't his intent. Before I knew it, he grabbed a hold of me. I was no match for his grown-man power and strength.*

The Roots of Infidelity Go DEEEEP

All I can recall is him forcing himself on top of me while holding his hand over my mouth. The more I struggled, the weaker I became. When he was done, he said, "If you say one damn word, I will **hurt** you!" *Fear was present in the worst way. He walked me back to the cabin where the others were still fast asleep. As we parted ways, he reminded me,* "If you say **ONE** word…" *He didn't need to remind me, though. I was absolutely terrified of what he would do to me **AND** what others would think about me if I told. I kept my mouth shut.*

The next day, as we prepared to leave, everyone could sense something was wrong with me. No one — not even the other adults present — took the time to ask, "What's the matter?" *I was left to feel like they knew what happened. I later learned there were a few of us who had similar experiences with Pastor Mike.*

*Being molested by a man at the age of 13 was the weirdest feeling imaginable. Nightmares became regular. I needed and desperately wanted to rid myself of the horrors related to that experience. Resentment for the church as a whole began to set in. Each week, we would go there at least two to three times for one thing or another. I couldn't understand why my aunt continued attending that church after what happened to me (in my young mind, I just **KNEW** she knew).*

After the incident, not only did I believe the other boys knew, I had to watch as Pastor Mike walked around the church with others praising the ground he walked on. My aunt couldn't stop talking about how much she enjoyed his vision for the church. Each time she said that, I would squirm. My uncle didn't go to church because he wasn't moved by the big hats and fake smiles he would receive when he did attend. My aunt and uncle filled the role as my parents, but nothing could take the place of having my birth parents active in my life. I felt that if they were around, Pastor Mike would have never molested me. No mom. No dad. A fake pastor preaching love and peace to the souls of his flock. I couldn't shake the thought of other men in the church possibly looking at me in a sexual manner as that of Pastor Mike.

Making sure I wasn't giving off any vibes other than being attracted to girls, I wanted to cleanse myself of the mental scars, even if that meant playing house or accepting Darlene allowing her little brother to have sex with her on a regular. I craved the attention from girls in any way they would give it to me to "give me back my manhood".

The Roots of Infidelity Go DEEEEP

THE WARNING SIGNS WERE THERE!

Many of you won't understand how difficult it is to rid yourself of mental scars. On one hand, you may recognize how the issues of your past have made you into the person you are today; however, the mind is something you can't easily patch up. You can readjust your focus. You can even do your best to forgive yourself and others who have hurt you in one way or another. On the other hand, if you would take the wool from over your eyes and see what's in front of you, you may find yourself truly amazed at how interconnected your life is with others and their experiences.

Ken found it challenging to see how people would continue to ignore the warning signs of destruction…

While still dealing with the emotional and mental stresses of all that happened to him that year, my Big Momma passed away. Damn! What else can possibly go wrong? I wanted **OUT***. I wanted out of the thoughts and feelings of being alone. I found myself attaching to anything that would take my mind off of the recent past events. Considering that time stands* *still for no one, it was soon time for me to start high school.*

The first day was exciting and terrifying at the same time. I was looking forward to new beginnings and all that came with them. I felt very confident in the looks department and knew I could hold down my own. I had spent all summer working out, played every sport possible, and stayed in shape. The girls who knew me made me feel wanted, but I wanted something new. Not only was I embarking on a new school with new people; I was getting ready to take a journey that would soar me farther away from everything negative.

I remember walking through the commons area during lunch when I spotted the most beautiful girl I had ever seen. I needed to know who she was. She smiled at me from across the way, which stopped me dead in my tracks. Not only did I need to know who she was, I needed her to want me. Hell, if she gave me a shot, I knew I had a chance to make things right in my sordid mind.

I approached her. "Hi. I'm Ken."

In the most seductive high school voice, she replied, "I know who you are."

The Roots of Infidelity Go DEEEEP

I was tickled pink. The butterflies in my stomach were fluttering like crazy! Smiling from ear to ear, I asked, "How do you know? And better yet, allow me to **FORMALLY** introduce myself!" *(I heard that line on TV somewhere.) When she smiled at my boyish remark, I couldn't believe a pick-up line from TV worked!*

She told me her name was Chasity. The way she said her name was mind-blowing. "Nice to meet you, Ken."

It was like a dream come true in many ways — bad in others. I was already talking to other girls. I wasn't dating anyone seriously, but I would gladly cut off all of them for her. I knew I hadn't seen her in any of my classes, so I had no idea what grade she was in. In my most vulnerable way, I asked her what grade she was in. That was a dead giveaway for her that I was either new to the school or a freshman. She laughed and said, "You **MUST** be a freshman." *Not knowing the full future impact of my question, she kindly and maturely stated she was a senior. Immediately, I saw my hopes flush down the drain. I knew there was no way I had a chance with her.*

I quickly stood my ground and said, "Yes, I am a freshman, but I didn't realize my age or grade had anything to do with me walking you to class."

Impressed by the boldness of my response, she replied, "Oh, he has a little game I see! I will have to watch out for you".

"Watch me now and anytime you'd like hereafter. You got this, and you don't even know it!"

Almost immediately, I cut all the other girls **OFF**. *Still, how in the world was I going to pull this one off? I mean, everyone knew I wasn't the 'commitment' type. My mind was saying one thing, but my life was saying another. Not wanting to pull the trigger one way or another, I allowed this thing to play itself out.*

After our initial meeting, we spoke on the phone many times. She even came to many of my football games. In fact, she was the one to drop me off at home after each game she attended. She worked a lot and appeared to have a lot going on after work. We would see each other as often as we could. Our time together didn't interfere with any of the other girls I knew (per se) because they were either freshmen or went to other schools.

The Roots of Infidelity Go DEEEEP

*I remember there being a local fair one weekend. On Saturday night, she was going out with her friends to a particular nightclub. I was too young to go, so I opted for the fair. While there, I ran into her cousins. One of them was dating my homeboy who was with me. Of course, he was trying to spend some 'quality time' with his girl and, since I had the house to myself, it wasn't long after that we made the way to my place. Chasity would be coming over soon, so everything worked out perfectly. When we arrived, my boy and his girl couldn't wait to get it in. I was left to entertain Chasity's other cousin, Tori, who began flirting with me. I played it off by ignoring her comments about me being so fine and how her big cousin was lucky to have me. Now, mind you: Tori was fine as hell. Damn, she was **FINE** – but there was **NO** way I could entertain that lust for even one millisecond. As we sat across from each other, her legs peeked open just enough for me to get a glimpse of the red thong she was wearing. I couldn't help but notice, as the sundress she had on clung to her body in such a way, everyone could see what was going on underneath. I told myself not to look, but man…it was hard not to! The thought of Chasity momentarily left my mind, and my body reacted. I snapped out of it and said,* "You know I can't get down with you like that. I'm dating your cousin."

"I know. That's why she can't find out," *was her reply.*

WHAT? *You mean she was ready to give me all of that and didn't want her cousin to find out?*

In the blink of an eye, Tori hopped across the space that separated us. She got a quick, firm grip on my penis after extracting it from the waistband of my sweatpants and put me inside of her. As soon as we were done, I was filled with guilt. I headed to the bathroom to clean myself up. When I exited, I was hopeful that the other two were still getting it in. ***NOPE!*** *They were sitting in the living room with a "knowing" look. As fate would have it, Tori told Chasity all about it. She never spoke to me again.*

Going through high school and knowing I messed things up with Chasity, I chalked it up to thinking it wasn't going to work between us. Our age difference made it hard for me to compete anyway.

My mom moving back home made things tough for me, too. After her long-term absence from my life, it took some adjusting to get used to having her around every day.

The Roots of Infidelity Go DEEEEP

One ordinary Saturday morning, I woke up, rubbed the sleep from my eyes, and made my way to the bathroom to relieve myself and brush my teeth. Rushing as if I was going to miss something, I couldn't wait to catch the morning news, hoping to see some of my football highlights from Friday night's game.

The walls were thin enough for me to hear my mom getting out of bed. Thinking nothing of it at first, I saw a tall man in one of my mom's robes walk out of her room. Then, I quickly sat up and thought, "Who in the hell is this in my house?" *Shortly after, his mom walked out in another one of her robes and said,* "Good morning, son!"

"Good morning."

Mom introduced me to her "good friend", Dalton. He shot me a quick, uninterested "Hello", *and then acted like he was all into the news. Mom must have thought I was still eight years old and dumb. Why was her "good friend" coming out of her bedroom with nothing on but a much-too-small robe? Wasn't it just two weeks prior when her "good friend", Al, was over?*

"Son, do you want some breakfast?"

*"Yes, ma'am." She knew I was hungry and that having her make me breakfast was our 'thing' on the weekends. Why **wouldn't** I be hungry?*

*While waiting for the food to finish cooking, Dalton took out what appeared to be weed. Next thing I knew, he and my mom were smoking and laughing hysterically. "Son, I better not catch you smoking this stuff!" My mouth responded with, "Yes, ma'am," but my **thoughts** were screaming,* **"SERIOUSLY? NOW YOU WANT TO BE A MOTHER?"** *My appetite left with the smoke that was lifting up through the air and I left the two to their antics.*

As I think back on those days and all the experiences I had in my life, it bothers me when I see how baffled parents are when their children turn out dysfunctional. How quickly they forget how their actions as parents truly mess with a child.

Time passed, and I was back on the prowl. I had a few new encounters and bedded different girls, but I remained uncommitted. My past still troubled me. Karma came to visit a few times, as well. The women I did truly like all played their roles very well. I had not a clue that some of them were seeing someone else. They made me feel like I was the only one. Talk about

The Roots of Infidelity Go DEEEEP

not being in touch with life! All throughout high school, my trust for others – not just girls – went out the window.

*As an adult, I see how deceitful people can be. In my mind, **all** women cheat and could not be trusted.*

*I did have one notable adult relationship where I gave it my all and was dealt a very bad hand (karma again, I suppose). As quiet as it was kept, I desired to be married and have children. The relationship I had with Candice was going well. Sure, we had challenges in the beginning (much like most relationships), but we worked our way through them. After many arguments, we reached a compromise we could both live with, only to later learn the deceit was **REAL**.*

Would Ken and Candice make it?

> *"Do not be anxious about anything, but in everything by prayer and supplication with thanksgiving let your requests be made known to God."*
>
> Philippians 4:6-7

The Roots of Infidelity Go DEEEEP

WHAT ABOUT ME?

Ken had other siblings on his dad's side. Candice, on the other hand, had both of her parents who were still married. Ken's dad left his mom years ago after infidelity crept into their relationship. The story he had been told for so long was that his mom was the cheater. Without his dad in the home, raising himself to be a man came by trial and error. His mom was always working two or three jobs at a time. His dad made every excuse he could not to spend time with his son. That wasn't the problem for Ken as much as the relationships his father had with his siblings. Having a father who spent more time with other children weighed heavily on his mind.

His mom didn't make it any better. Every chance she had, she would point out that his dad was doing something with his other children. *"Your dad can't come today because he took his other children to 'this place' or 'that place'."* Unaware of the depths of envy at the time, Ken grew up resenting his siblings for the things his dad did. He could remember many holidays when all of them would be forced to occupy the same space while Ken watched how his siblings were treated better than he was. He constantly felt like the stepchild, even though he was the oldest. Seeing them receive gifts he never did or being taken places he could only dream of placed a huge strain on the relationship with his dad.

His dad's wife wanted nothing to do with Ken. When Ken was an adult and able to form relationships with his siblings, he learned that their mothers poisoned their brains with a hatred for Ken. They recalled when his name was mentioned, or he would come over, their mom instructed them to not speak to Ken—unless they wanted to. She even went so far as to plant a seed of doubt, stating that she wasn't even sure Ken was truly their kinfolk, as Ken's mom was known to run the streets a lot. Who would tell kids something like that, right? The dynamics of blended families have truly been a silent epidemic that has plagued many households.

You might ask, *"How does that contribute to infidelity?"* Well, that factor alone could be a driving force for many to seek a way of escape.

Men, consider the woman you meet who has children. Naturally, questions arise. *"Where is*

The Roots of Infidelity Go DEEEEP

the child's father?" "Are all the children by the same man?" Depending on the answer to those questions, your perception of that woman can be altered from the start. In either case, you start spending time together and fall in love. The time comes for the children to be introduced to you. Will they like you? Will you like them? That unspoken hurdle looms oddly like a pine tree growing in the middle of a desert. The children have been taught to respect adults, so the meeting and interactions are always cordial at best. However, we can all remember a time or two when our parents did something that our young minds didn't know how to process. Taking all factors into consideration, a once-promising relationship can take a turn for the worse when you start to peel back the layers of challenges that can potentially arise when you try to blend families.

On the surface, the relationship between you and the children's mother is great! Sex? Outstanding! Fun times? Check! When the child dynamic is introduced, you may find yourself questioning if that's how you want to spend the rest of your life. During that questioning phase, you may find yourself allowing your mind to wander.

You have a night out on the town with the fellas and meet someone who doesn't have children. That woman may fill your immediate need of being the **ONLY** apple of one's eye. Do you cut off the one you've already formed a relationship with? Do you test the waters? Do you start over? They are all legitimate questions asked in your secret thoughts, yet you find yourself waiting to see if the outcome will push you in a particular direction—even if deep down inside, you know it's not the correct path.

Ken had so many scars to deal with that added to the layers of challenging dynamics between him and Candice. Can you imagine entering into a marriage without ever addressing them? What about having children and raising them under the mindset of being hated by their other 'outside' siblings? Unspoken dynamics turn the key to 'ON' of the 'Cheatmobile'.

Candice felt that it was important for a man to take care of her financially. She was raised in a home where dad always worked, and mom stayed home. While seeing her mom wake up every morning to make sure her dad was okay, Candice felt that when she ever met a man, he had to live up to the standards that were being set by her father.

For Candice, she didn't make the connection of how her remarks fueled their arguments. *"Be a man, Ken!"* or *"My dad says I should probably do 'this'."* Unbeknownst to Candice, she was stripping away Ken's identity as a man little by little. He found himself asking if he could truly be the man she wanted or was he secretly competing with her father. When talks of finances came into question, the idea of being a man fled with each day that marched by and he was unable to find a job. He went through a 12-week period, not having any income to claim as his own. During that time, he relied heavily on Candice to pay their bills. Each argument started with the accusatory, *"What did you do today?"* That alone would trigger a nerve. She didn't see Ken wake up every day and submit no less than 75 resumes and applications online.

She could not understand why it was so hard for him to find a job. She didn't know that not meeting her needs and not contributing financially like he did in the beginning of their relationship would bother him. The constant bickering and verbal punches thrown were tough to deal with. Rather than support him in a moment of trouble, he felt attacked. All the while, Candice felt that if she had to struggle with a man, she might as well struggle alone. As both saw the validity of their own point of view, they failed to see the other's point of view. The unspoken and assumed expectations proved to be challenging.

God forbid Joseph or Pat called. That, too, would cause another set of issues. Ken just needed to get away. Candice felt he could be using that 'time away' to seek employment. If nothing else, she felt he shouldn't spend money loosely if she is struggling to maintain.

What if Ken spoke to her and told her how he felt? What if Candice said she didn't want to feel like she was taking care of both of them? Like most couples, talking seems too much like the right thing to do. Arguments begin to appear like they are the most beneficial way to reach a solution. Think about it. Could it be changed?

The Roots of Infidelity Go DEEEEP

WAIT A MINUTE! YOU'RE WHAT?

After a very heated argument one evening, Ken was close to calling it quits.

At 5:30 a.m., the clock sounded its alarm. Ken couldn't believe how quickly the morning came. After being up most of the night arguing with Candice, he hurried to the shower, hoping that would wake him up. While showering, he recalled everything that was said and tried to process it. The words she spoke were very hurtful. Opting not to address it further, he knew it was best to get out of the house before she started up again. When he exited the shower, Candice was sitting in the chair in the bathroom holding his towel. *"We need to talk,"* she said. As he reached for his towel, he took a deep breath and exhaled loudly.

"What do we need to talk about at 5:45 in the morning, Candice? Didn't you criticize me enough last night?"

"Ken, I know my words hurt your feelings, but that was not my intention," she replied while looking at him in the mirror.

He took a moment to respond, as he tried to calm down from the anger that started to rise. *"It's never your intention, Candice. Never. Yet, we always find ourselves here."*

She reached her hand out to grab his. Holding his hand firmly and speaking with a subtle voice, she reassured him by saying, *"Ken, I'm sorry. I know I have to work on some things, but I love you and didn't mean it"*. She continued speaking in a quiet voice but found it difficult to complete a sentence. *"Ken, last night…"*

"Last night what, Candice? You keep doing the same thing over and over when we set aside time to be with one another."

Her eyes began to water. *"Ken, you are not listening to me. I wasn't…"*

"Wasn't what, Candice? Wasn't concerned about how I felt?"

In full-blown tears, she continued. *"I can't talk to you because you never listen to me."*

The Roots of Infidelity Go DEEEEP

One of their man issues was the inability to communicate. Both felt they had to get their point across at any cost.

Becoming angry and defensive, he said, *"Okay.* ***TALK****, Candice. I will let you say whatever it is you have to say"*.

She took a moment to calm down and wipe her tears away. *"When I told you I didn't care about your feelings or even when I said you don't have to cook for me, it wasn't because I was ungrateful."*

He took a seat next to her after tiring of standing, looked down at the floor, and said, *"Um-hmm"* every three words. Nodding his head throughout Candice's explanation of why she didn't eat, he failed to listen to anything she was saying. He was operating out of the hurt he felt. *"Um-hmm, um-hmm, um-hmm"* was all he was willing to give to acknowledge she was speaking.

Frustrated by his lack of attention, she asked, *"Ken, what did I just say?"* Looking shocked and aggravated at the same time, he replied, *"You said you didn't eat the food I prepared for you because…"*

"Because of what, Ken? Were you even paying attention to me when I told you I'm pregnant?"

Shocked and in disbelief, he asked for clarification. *"Wait. We're having a baby?"* She was silent. *"Candice, are we having a **baby**?"*

She grabbed his hand and placed it on her belly. *"Yes. **THIS** is why it has been difficult for me to eat the spicy foods you always make for me."*

Feeling genuinely horrible for his bad attitude, he exclaims, *"Baby, I'm truly sorry. I'm so happy! I've always wanted you to have my…wait…**OUR** baby!"*

He felt an obligation to explain his actions. *"Look, Candice. Today was a very hard day. I couldn't stop thinking about how we got here. I want to first address something you hate hearing about. When I think about the situation for what it is, my blood boils because I feel you are downplaying what is really going on. I've come to accept it for what it is. No man on earth wants to feel as if he isn't good enough. My thoughts are all over the place. My mind can't stop wondering about what the real issue is.*

The Roots of Infidelity Go DEEEEP

"The point is this: I feel like I put too much of my feelings into this relationship too soon. My friends think I did, too. For me, I feel like I'm not getting any younger, so when you came into my life, and I knew I wanted to be with you, why not share my true feelings?

"I couldn't help that I was fired for being honest on the job. I told management I wasn't in agreement with how they handled the situation with the lady they fired weeks ago. I believe that's the reason they let me go, although I was released under the guise of 'downsizing'. All the lady said was that she struggled with the lack of diversity within the job. It's a true statement. Aside from her, there's hardly any women, let alone minorities, in leadership positions. Should I have lied? I know that's not the issue, but if I didn't have any principles, what would be the purpose?

"I know I bring a lot of baggage into our relationship. I know I do. I've exposed some of that baggage at the wrong times, which puts you on pause. I accept that. I'm so consumed with all kinds of thoughts, it surreal at times.

"I've been angry all day when I think about you because I allowed myself to be mind-fucked by you. I believed in you, Candice. I really did. I also see how I *smothered you as well. I wanted all of your time and didn't think there would be a problem, yet it was. I enjoyed every moment with you. So, when I hear words like "smother" and "not being a man", it's a punch in the gut. True as it may be, it messed with my head. I never thought we would be here. I sincerely wanted to be everything you ever needed and wanted. There are times I look at you and feel secure in how you feel about me. Other times, it seems as though you're settling just because of the nice way I treat you. Your actions – not what you say – lead me to those thoughts. I know I'm not your "type". At the end of the day, it doesn't matter how I treat you; you will always want what you want. For me, I know I've tried too hard to prove something to you – which showed in the ignorance of my actions.*

"When I woke up this morning, I started the process of removing myself from your life – not because I don't want to be in it but because I don't think you want "me". I asked God all day, "Why?" If one of the issues you have with me is me being faithful or anything along those lines, I can promise you: that is not an issue. I can work on the other stuff. But what I don't want is to be told I am not a man constantly.

"I am unemployed, Candice. There is a huge difference between being unemployed and being a man.

The Roots of Infidelity Go DEEEEP

I desire to take care of you because I want to, not because of what your dad did for you. I always tell you: If you want to be with a man like your father, that's not me. I am who I am. Look, all I'm trying to say is this: I love you unconditionally and hope we can work through our issues because now, we have a child to take care of."

"I hear you, Ken. I swear I do. The problems I have are not that you aren't a man, even though I said it. It's more about me not being able to see where you're motivated, and that scares me. Not to mention the arguments we've had that turned into physical altercations. Do you know how hard those things make this? What I love about my dad is that no matter what my mom did or said, he never put his hands on her."

"But you slapped me first, Candice!"

"It doesn't matter, Ken."

That statement right there causes so much trouble in relationships. No man should ever hit a woman, but how many times does a woman put her hands on a man before he reacts?

Ken continued. *"The hardest thing for me is realizing how unnecessary the fights were. They were beyond pointless. I'm ashamed in so many ways. The very thing I despise in men, I did. You could have slapped me over the head with a bat a million times over; I shouldn't have grabbed your hair or put my hands around your neck. We are two adults battling each other instead of loving each other. There are so many things we both have to work on, even if we aren't in each other's life. I feel like I hit rock bottom with you that night. That look on your face? I never wanted to bring you to a place that reminded you of your past. Everything that was negative in your life, I wanted to counter them with positivity. Unfortunately, it came with irritating you and me losing my job – which made you feel insecure in my ability to provide. That's on me. For that, I apologize.*

"All I want is what's best for you, even if that doesn't include me. I'm sure there are a lot of relationships that make it through things like this, but it should not become the norm. I can't make you want this or me. I can't force you to try and make it work. I just don't think we put our all into it properly to give it a fair chance. Yes, I wished you would have expressed things a little more, but it's not who you are. You show me things in different ways, and it's cool.

"From the very bottom of my heart, I wished we could have had a long future. I want to believe I

The Roots of Infidelity Go DEEEEP

mean more to you than what you said to and about me last night. Selfishly, it's somewhat helping me cope. Still, I have to be realistic and see things for what they are. No one wants to go through breakups or fights. As I stated, if we mean what we said we meant, we will overcome this — along with other issues."

"Let what you say be simply 'Yes' or 'No'; anything more than this comes from evil."

Matthew 5:37

The Roots of Infidelity Go DEEEEP

THE "SHIFT"

After listening to and absorbing all that Ken had to say, it was time for Candice to share her truths. She was prayerful he would be just as receptive as she was…

"Before meeting you, I was just living life. It was almost as if I was living with no purpose. I was angry and tired of living the life of being perfect in the sight of my parents or anyone else, for that matter. It was becoming old to me. I felt I disobeyed God by living a lie. However, I never gave up on trying to talk and listen to God.

"I remember sitting at home – angry, unhappy, and miserable. I was honestly at a point of just saying "Screw it all!" *and never be in a relationship again because I didn't want to deal with the bullcrap anymore. I met many men, yet not one of them made me want to do things differently. That same day, as I sat at home all up in my feelings, I tried talking to God. I simply said to Him,* "If you allow the man I need in my life to cross my path, I will never go back to my ways and will do my part in trying to help others, just as I know you would want me to do."

When I met you, I was in awe because it was as if you popped up out of nowhere. Sure, all I saw was a handsome man at first. That night when I left the club, I felt different than I have ever before. I told you it was my first time there. I wasn't even supposed to go to that particular club that night.

"Then, after talking to you on the phone, meeting to get a bite to eat, and the time we spent together immediately after, I knew this was the lane I should be in, regardless of my upbringing. What I was not prepared for was meeting you where you were mentally.

"I can only use my experiences as a guide to understanding this situation I have with you. I can't explain it, but I somewhat get it. It's almost like the timing was off. Understanding you is not as difficult as it seems in many ways. Now, there are still things I do not understand, but I'm hoping that will come with time. Listening to all that you have been through, I concluded that you are at a crossroad in your life.

"To help you sleep at night, you need a sense of financial security. I get it. It is almost like a person struggles their whole life and finally makes it, doing whatever it takes never to go back there again. I could be wrong, but that is how I see you. On both the

The Roots of Infidelity Go DEEEEP

financial and relationship fronts, you have been burned before. People have broken your trust and, for you, the only way to feel okay in your mind is to protect yourself by any means necessary. In protecting yourself, you realize that some may get hurt along the way, but you need to make sure you are safe first. You want to be financially-happy and in a relationship, so you struggle with finding and accepting both.

*"You did not expect to meet me. You did not expect to grow close to me so fast. In fact, that part scares you a lot because not only did you grow close to me, you grew close to a person you weren't even sure of. I'm sure you thought I had an ulterior motive. My truth is that I believe in my heart God sent you to me. I cannot predict the future. Hell, we all would operate differently if we could! However, what I can tell you is that through all your fears, emotions, and whatever else, I want and will be beside you through it all. I want you to be **MORE** than happy. I want you to be free from all things that make you lose sleep.*

"It's almost as if we both are enduring things from our past in this relationship. I think there is something we should be learning through it all as individuals – if that makes sense. My insecurities stem from my past and some of the things that have happened between us. I know my areas of weakness:

You want a woman who is secure in herself, who you can have fun with, and makes your life easier. I know I am not perfect, but I'm hoping I'm perfect for you."

That very moment, their relationship shifted for the better.

Ken never knew how she truly felt until then. Unsure if her moment of transparency was due to the pregnancy or what, they were words he'd been waiting to hear—and he embraced them. Joseph and Pat didn't think the two of them would make it, but they did! It wasn't because Candice was pregnant; it was because both learned they desired to be better individuals.

The Roots of Infidelity Go DEEEEP

LOYALTY? WHAT'S THAT?

Having done so much in his life, Joseph is easily sickened when he sees the blatant cheating with no regard. No one seemed to care about who else it affected but themselves. There are so many people he knew who refuse to deal with their broken issues.

Tim and Jana are good friends of Joseph. Jana refused to let go of what Tim did. You see, a few years back, Tim stepped out on his wife and had sex with one of her so-called friends.

Jana stopped talking to her friend long ago because Jana saw how disloyal that woman was by sleeping with other women's husbands and boyfriends. As long as Jana could recall, her former friend never dated anyone who was single. Jana knew what she was and chose to distance herself from her, yet Tim fell victim to his demons and had a one-night stand with that trick.

The night it happened, Tim was mad at Jana. He got dressed and went out with the fellas. After a few hours, Tim was the only one left at the bar, as his friends left on a party bus headed to the strip club. Tim knew that going with them would have been taking it too far, so he stayed behind and nursed one more drink. Next thing he knew, Jana's friend (at the time) walked up to the bar and had a seat next to Tim.

Tim always talked about how fine that woman was. Every time, Joseph would tell him that he will find himself in trouble if he kept thinking those lustful thoughts. As sure as the day turns to night, what happened? Tim fell for it. Of course, he blamed it on the alcohol, but as many times as he mentioned how fine she was, the opportunity presented itself, and he went for broke.

Now, after Tim's cheating, Jana chose to stick it out and work through the issue. They went to counseling and the whole nine yards, but for whatever the reason, Jana turned into the nagging wife no man wants. Tim tried giving her the space and time she needed to heal and forgive him, but he soon grew tired of the nagging. It was apparent Jana wasn't ready to heal, and rather than deal with that issue, she was self-destructing. She fueled Tim's inner demon—the one that lied to him and had him believing he was free from the other demons that plagued him. He started hanging out more and more to avoid the incessant nagging at home.

For Tim and Jana, their days became so routine and toxic, the number of cheating incidents continued to multiply.

Dewayne Williams

"A man of many companions may come to ruin, but there is a friend who sticks closer than a brother."

Proverbs 18:24

The Roots of Infidelity Go DEEEEP

SECRETS EXPOSED

Joseph, being the 'seasoned one' in the group, could always revert back to something that happened in his past relationships. Joseph recalled a time when he learned just how bad secrets can destroy any relationship...

It was a Wednesday morning, and as soon as the alarm clock went off, he hurried into the shower and immediately left the house. He was in no mood to force a conversation with his wife, and he damn sure didn't feel like enduring the awkward silence the two of them had been experiencing as of late. He made his normal calls to his crew—Paul, Ken, and Pat—which usually soaked up all of five minutes total. It was common for the four of them to make sure each was alright from the night before since each was dealing with problems at home.

For Paul, his wife had recently left him because he couldn't leave the drugs and alcohol alone. He started off smoking weed at least three times a day, but that wasn't the problem. He began drinking heavily and was introduced to heroin. It was then that things got really bad at home. Paul was spending entire paychecks on drugs. The drug abuse led to the abuse of his wife, Tessa.

Tessa called Joseph one night screaming into the phone. *"Paul beat me! Please help!"* When Joseph arrived, he found Paul in such a stoned state of mind, he didn't even realize what he had done to Tessa.

What was the root of Paul's issues? The deep dark secret that plagued his family for years was about to be exposed: The man he knew as his father killed his mother.

Paul went to visit his father in jail one Saturday morning. On that day, he learned that the man he knew as his father really wasn't his father.

So the story goes: When he was 16 years old, his mother and the man he knew to be his father were arguing. Apparently, one of his friends randomly-stated during an outing with a group of guys, *"You know Paul is MY son, right?"* Filled with confusion and rage, the man and

The Roots of Infidelity Go DEEEEP

Paul's father started fighting. Still filled with adrenaline, he then went home to confront Paul's mother. She confessed to sleeping with that man. Next thing, she was lying in a pool of blood. He had beaten her to death with his bare hands. When the police came, his father told them they were arguing about her cheating, but he left out the 'small' detail about Paul not being his son because of the indiscretion.

When Paul's 'father' was released from jail, it was then that he admitted he kept the secret from Paul because he was ashamed of what had taken place. His justification continued when he said, *"I didn't want you to have any negative thoughts about your mother."*

When Paul was finally told who his biological father was, he learned it was the man who he knew as his 'play uncle'. That man was heavily involved in drugs and Paul had no desire to pursue a relationship with him. Ironically, Paul turned to drugs as a way of escape. He seemed to be spiraling out of control, just as his now-deceased father did from an overdose.

Tessa felt the brunt of Paul's brokenness every day in one way or another. One day, when she couldn't take it anymore, she just up and left him.

The morning conversations between Joseph and Paul were primarily about finding a way to deal with Paul's issues **AND** get his wife back. The good thing was that Tessa didn't want a divorce. Tessa was raised by parents who instilled in her: Do whatever you can to save your marriage. Stand by your husband through thick and thin.

When she left Paul, Tessa moved in with her parents. She felt very neglected and alone. In talking with her, Joseph heard the pain in her voice when she expressed her need for affection and for her husband to get his life back on track. Joseph tried his hardest to help Paul, even as his own marriage was turning to shit.

Joseph's marriage soon settled in a 'new normal' Phone conversations became task-oriented. There was never any substance to them. If it wasn't about the children, it was about things that needed to be done around the house. The pattern had been in place for so long, when a regular conversation took place, it was extremely awkward.

Of course, that awkwardness spilled over into the bedroom. There was **NO** intimacy present. To make the best of the situation, she slept upstairs with the children, and Joseph slept downstairs on the couch. The children were none the wiser because, by the time he made it home, there was just enough time to tuck them in for the night. The 'new normal' gave him the opportunity to catch up on the news and unwind while also being able to communicate with whomever he desired without having her peek over his shoulder. That suited him just fine.

Interestingly enough, Joseph's marriage wasn't the only one with a 'new normal'.

> *"Think over what I say, for the Lord will give you understanding in everything."*
>
> 2 Timothy 2:7

A LITTLE BIT OF THIS…A LOT OF THAT

Bryan, another one of Joseph's friends, was going through the same thing as Joseph. He has been married for ten years; the relationship has been rocky for six of them. Bryan knew from day one the reputation his wife had, but he fell in love with her nonetheless and hoped marriage and children would change her. Unfortunately, things didn't change. In fact, they grew progressively worse over the years.

The level of disrespect Bryan's wife displayed towards him was unreal, from her talking to him as if he was some random guy on the street to her lack of affection and bitter means of communication. Things were so bad, she often had verbal confrontations with his mom. His wife's side of the family would dismiss her obvious lack of respect by saying, *"Oh, that's just the way she is"*. No one ever addressed her anger issues directly. She knew she had them, but her lack of dedication to get help was rooted in her pride.

What's a man to do?

Bryan grew up in Phoenix, Arizona where he was a very popular guy. From sports to his charming personality, he was truly an eye-catcher. While many women had their eyes on him, he always had a crush on his football coach's daughter, Andrea. Friends for almost the entire time they were in high school, he never said a word to her about his true feelings, as he felt their friendship was more important. After graduation, they stayed in touch via email and social media.

Bryan went to the University of California to study Finance. That's where he met his wife. Although she was **WELL**-known around campus as being loosey-goosey with her body, the two seemed to hit it off well. As time passed, the marriage they entered into came with so much potential. He anticipated things were going to be tough, which led him to where he was presently.

Bryan works for a major finance company as an Executive. He is constantly traveling and doing all he can to support his family. When he noticed things started to get progressively worse between he and his wife, he started to contemplate divorce and became extremely frustrated with the current state of the relationship.

One day while at work, his wife called and he made the mistake of answering it while his colleagues were within earshot. **"WHY IN THE HELL HAVEN'T YOU CALLED ME?"** came her loud voice, echoing throughout the room. In his calmest demeanor, he explained that he was in a meeting and would call her back. He was so embarrassed. He knew they heard her. As soon as he hung up the phone, he quickly apologized and laughed it off with, *"She was just joking."* He knew no one bought it, but he was sticking to his guns on that one.

That was the day he had enough. He didn't know what he was going to do, but he knew that wasn't the life he wanted for his children and him. Coincidently, that was the same day Andrea sent him an email asking how he was doing.

Always a private person, Bryan took a different approach and replied to her email by openly stating how frustrated he was. He didn't go into much detail, but it was enough to prompt Andrea to send her phone number along, asking him to call her. As soon as the workday came to a close, he instructed his assistant to hold all calls. He sat in silence in his office, mentally preparing himself to call Andrea. The two spoke for what seemed like hours. He opened up to her in such a way that Andrea offered to listen to him as often as he needed.

That one phone call altered his marriage in a very subtle way.

Bryan and Andrea lived in different states. He had an upcoming conference in Atlanta, Georgia, the city in which Andrea resided. The two planned on catching up in person when he arrived. With things being so bad at home, he told his wife that the meeting was for five days. The truth was that it was only for three. He extended his stay by two days to spend time with Andrea and forget about all the drama at home. Each night after the conference, the two would grab a bite to eat and have a drink.

Two days before he was scheduled to leave, the two shared their true feelings about one another. That led to them crossing a line that could never be undone. He made love to her in a way that made her feel like the queen she thought she was. In her heart, all she wanted was to see Bryan happy. She hated how frustrated his wife made him. She told Bryan she couldn't understand how a woman would **EVER** disrespect a man like him—and he fed right into those comforting words. He needed and appreciated her sensitivity. He needed her compassion. He needed her respect, and Andrea was all in. At the time, he hadn't slept with his wife for over a month. Andrea definitely filled **THAT** need.

When the day came for him to leave, it was bittersweet. More importantly, it was a moment of truth and clarity for their situation. Neither lived in the same city, so he couldn't just pick up a phone and call her any time of the day or night. The double-life he chose started the moment he landed, as he became very calculating in what he did and how he did it.

As time passed, feelings between the two blossomed. He wanted more of what Andrea had to offer and much less of what his wife was dishing out. He soon found himself compartmentalizing his life. He was a father for a few hours, an executive for the bulk of the day, an unhappy husband, and a fulfilled little boy with Andrea. The urgency to rid himself of his marriage grew daily, but he didn't want to leave his children. Neither of them wanted a divorce — per se; they just didn't want each other. The more time that passed, the more Andrea wanted him. Her eagerness was growing out of control as the weeks and then months went by.

For Andrea, all she was looking for was a good man. What she wanted was a single man, yet she found herself falling in love with a married one. She wanted children and a family of her own, but always had difficulty grasping those things. The men she would come across were never as polite and respectful as Bryan. For her, Bryan was a breath of fresh air. She had convinced herself that having a piece of man was better than having no man at all.

The cycle of her and Bryan's lives went through so many emotional roller coaster rides. They even planned a life together once his divorce was final. Still, she was torn every night. She knew she was the other woman. She also knew she hated having it thrown in her face by

The Roots of Infidelity Go DEEEEP

something said in a movie, through random conversations, or something sung on the radio. The sting of being the other woman caused tension between her and Bryan on many days. She knew he was married, but her wants and needs remained unfulfilled by him as well.

The moral of the story here is simple: The roots of infidelity affect everyone. Honesty is not enough, but it's a start. Making a conscious decision to step away from any relationship should be done with fairness and a clean slate. Bringing another into the mix is unfair — whether or not that person is a willing participant. Lastly, always remember that people have lost their lives for much less. With infidelity being the root of issues for many relationships, choose **NOW** to address it.

~~~~~~~~~~

Did Pat and Brandy make it work? Should they keep trying?

Would Tim and Jana outgrow their ways?

Did Tessa hold on, or did Paul's actions cause her to stray from her upbringing?

"For we must all appear before the judgment seat of Christ, so that each one may receive what is due for what he has done in the body, whether good or evil."

2 Corinthians 5:10

CONCLUSION

Infidelity. What is it *exactly*? A hook-up? Paid sex? A massage with a 'happy ending'? Masturbation with thoughts of someone else? Monogamy has always been defined as being with one person forever; however, in today's society, it's viewed as being with one person at a time—regardless of the length of time. The very act of sex has become trivialized for many. It's more in line with achieving that next climax and nothing more. There are no real intimate pleasures anymore. Foreplay is practically obsolete. The sexual positions in the bedroom have become ordinary. There is no real *connection* to one's mate, other than obligation or duty to perform. Sex is almost looked down upon, as it shouldn't be talked about openly with others (and for good reason). So many people are struggling with intimacy in their relationships. Even if they are loyal to their mate *physically*, many wander off *mentally*.

What then? What is the solution?

For me, it's simple: Tear down the walls that have been set in place and verbalize whatever it is that's on your mind. Don't hold

anything back. Whatever you are feeling, say ***THAT***!

In retrospect, I acknowledge the issues will not be fixed overnight. Still, I can't help but cringe at the thought of how foul people can be when it comes to infidelity. One-night trysts are now being praised as if it literally makes you a king or queen, yet arguments arise when one's morals are challenged. Crazy! To make it worse, some have found themselves "falling in love" with one-night stands. Delusional! Think about it.

You never know what people are going through. Like Joseph, you may have several friends or family members who have gone through similar situations addressed on the pages of this book. In either case, everyone must take accountability for his or her own actions.

Women - Stop sleeping with men and telling them: *"This is yours!" "Don't leave me!" "Ooooo…it feels so good. You're the BEST!"* It's "only his" when it benefits you, and a new Gucci purse is a part of the deal. *"Don't leave me"* is a cry for wanting only him in the moment. ***Sidebar:*** How can you ask a man not to leave you when he's cheating **with** you? Telling him he's the "best" feeds his ego and keeps the momentum of the vicious cycle of infidelity ongoing. It's almost scary to think about how many times women have used those words with *EVERY* man they've been with.

Men – Stop making excuses for your inability to grow up. If there is an issue you have as a man, address it! Stop going through the *motions* of a relationship when you are in the presence of your mate, and then acting single when you're not. If you are in a relationship and only you and a few of your close friends know it, something is **terribly** wrong. If all you and your 'boys' talk about are other women, one of two things are happening or need to happen: 1. You *want* to hear about and connect with other women outside the boundaries of your relationship or 2. You need to find a new circle of friends who add *value* to your life.

Often, we never truly evaluate the circle we find ourselves in as it relates to the people we call 'friends'. Just as with monogamous relationships, it is the same for friendships in that we typically attract those things in which we are weak or don't want to address. Those things hinder us from seeing what we need to see and being who we need to be. There are many 'Josephs' running around with a group of friends who are dealing with some deep-rooted issues. Many people (not just men; not just women) make a conscious choice to step outside of their relationship, but do we ever consider other contributing factors, such as the company we keep? If you are hanging with friends and find yourself flirting with the idea of breaking that monogamous tie, would the company you keep encourage you to turn away from the temptation **or** will they become the catalyst to your future excuses of doing the wrong thing? Ideally, your circle should **always** push you to remain faithful to the principles of being in a monogamous relationship.

We all want loyalty. We all want that perfectly-fitting "pair of shoes", but in order for us to be loyal in a relationship, we must first be loyal to who we are. Ask yourself these questions: *Have I given my all to the relationship* (meaning have you asked your mate about his or her needs **and** are meeting those needs)? *Have I been unselfish in this relationship? Have I fought tooth and* *nail for my relationship?* Now, those questions are for a union in which the couple feels they are meant to be—not the relationship that people hold on to for the sake of saying they are "committed" to one another. If you can answer 'yes' without hesitation, then the final question I pose is this: *Have you turned a blind eye to something you know you should have addressed?* An example might be when you look into your mate's eyes, do you **truly** feel what you say you feel? The overall point is to dig **DEEEEP** and ask yourself, ***"What have I done for the sake of this relationship?"***

When we consider all the other challenges of life, one might ask, **"Why add more to it?"** There are people in this world who struggle with not having a relationship with their parents. Hell, some don't even know their biological parents. Many that are in interracial relationships find themselves struggling with being accepted by closed-minded in-laws. Far more people struggle with their sexual identity. The list goes on and on. To think that we would ***intentionally*** add fuel to those deep-rooted issues by cheating, how could a person ever handle the added burden? As I'm sure you are aware, people have lost their lives behind infidelity in relationships. Whether it be intentional or unintentional, it's real out here; yet, we walk around acting as if it doesn't happen and take unnecessary risks. If we are honest, at one point in our lives, we condoned infidelity of a family member or friend. And for what? Because we, too, were stuck on nonsense!

If we honestly took a step back away from it all and removed alliances and the idea of us thinking we know what someone will or won't do, we would truly understand that anyone is capable of doing anything (even if that means hurting someone close to them). The power of selfishness is stronger than that of submitting — in all senses of the word.

Some of us grew up in a household where we held our parents to a very high regard. They gave us the best quality of life we knew to be. They shielded us from their selfishness is many ways, as they didn't want us to see what was really taking place behind the bedroom walls: unhappiness! In their minds, they thought they were doing the right thing by not involving children in their affairs. I'm sure if you were given the opportunity to see what was really

The Roots of Infidelity Go DEEEEP

happening, the view of your parents would be different.

Have you ever considered how maybe you were what tore them apart? Take, for example, your parents initially agreed to have one or two children. Life went on, and one of your parents remained in the home "for the sake of the kid(s)". They were very unhappy for a variety of reasons. For the sake of argument, we will say that your dad was extremely unhappy with your mom. In his mind, he felt your mom was controlling. He could never go anywhere without it being an issue. She nagged him about everything. She always complained that he could never do anything right. In her mind, she was tired of your dad cheating on her. While she wanted her family, the only way she knew how to respond was by venting in the most uncomfortable ways (hear your dad tell it). So, both continue with their duties as husband/wife, father/mother. They went through the motions for many years.

Time passes, and your mom is pregnant with you. In both of their minds, they knew they were only there because of your sibling(s), and both knew they only had a few years left of obligation in rearing your sibling(s). Can you imagine the sense of feeling trapped on both parts now, even if one was intentional about the pregnancy with hopes that the new birth would keep them together? So, here you come into the world. What was once only a few years left of coping is now 18 more years of the back and forth. Not convinced?

The challenge that many of us, even as adults, don't consider is the struggle our parents endured. It is important that we understand that unhappiness has no boundary. No one is exempt from riding that emotional roller coaster. The cycle of life continues to go on, and one thing I can promise is that if you live long enough, you will begin to see things for what they are.

Up and down, twisting and turning goes the roller coaster of our lives. We play Russian Roulette with our own lives when we step outside of our relationships by never considering the potential consequences of our actions. In the blink of an eye, temptation and fornication take over. Some of us have signed a contract with the devil and don't even realize it. Even if you don't believe in the devil, you may have signed a mental contract with the intent on not caring about anyone other than yourself. Truth be told, when we are dealing with relationship issues, the **last** thing we want is "helpful advice". We simply want others to agree with the decisions we have made. We compare ourselves to so many things that when our mate is in our presence, we unfairly compare him or her to what we had previously. Again, we are wanting those things that cater to our weaknesses. Let that marinate for a minute…

No one wants or likes rejection; however, it will come whether we want it to or not. For me, it came at a very young age. That was a very hard pill to swallow, and I held onto it longer than I should have. It was the foundation for me treating women the way I did. I hoped one day I could get past it, but the truth was and remains that sometimes, you are never their first choice. No matter how hard you try to hide it, you simply cannot hide where your heart is. Unfortunately, the people who find themselves in a relationship they know they shouldn't be in are often an 'outlet' (to say the least). They are simply people you could talk to about almost anything, whatever the day brought forth. It often turns into something that was more of a pattern than anything else. You get used to talking to them, and before you know it, they become a constant in your life. You knew it was wrong from day one, yet you simply didn't care because you were in a dark place. The very moment you decided to deal with them, you devalued yourself. In your idle times of thought, you begin to question the integrity of everyone else. I mean, if you could deal with them knowing they are married, what in the hell makes you remotely think it could not or would not happen to you. It is as if we (people) play games with ourselves. You press towards the mark with the intentions of taking it for all that you could — and some go as far as leaving one relationship to enter into another! Then, when in that 'new' relationship, they question why trust is an issue. Rather than be clear on the intentions and expectations upfront, they disregard reality for a moment of deceit.

Being clear on expectations upfront can eliminate many conflicts in any relationship. Not knowing where someone stands on a particular issue can lead to many problems. For many men, he may feel he needs you in more ways than what is on the surface, meaning that he needs his woman to act like a lady, a queen, his everything. Rather than putting you on a pedestal, he places you where he feels you deserve to be. As the saying goes, "If he's into you, there will be no questioning that."

In the reverse, know and understand that when things are "off", they are "off". It will affect the relationship in ways that you think men are never affected. For example, just as women aren't turned on by certain things, so is the same for a man. If he sees you as his one and only, he may not respond affectionately or sexually — even if you find yourself thinking otherwise. So, no, he's not thinking about someone else per se; he is just in tune with you so much that he is affected by your words. Those words touch an emotional nerve that, as a woman, you could never understand. Take note: If a man tells you something affects him, it's deeper than what the surface may say. Given this, the same can be said as it relates to women as well. Many times, men don't do a good job of listening or paying attention to the small things that women need. When these things go unaddressed, it opens the door for fleeting thoughts to come in…and those are never good for any relationship. The art of any relationship is knowing what moves the other person. When you know what makes them tick, **MAKE THEM TICK**!

Know this: You cannot stop anyone from doing what they want to do. Your only job is to make sure you pay attention to the warning signs *AND* adhere to them. I'm not talking about wanting to leave when things get tough. I'm simply referring to when his or her attention is elsewhere. Even if neither of you are affectionate or have a need to cuddle underneath one another, if the two of you want what you have, just being in each other's presence will suffice. You will find yourselves enjoying doing things together, which is equally important. One key aspect of any successful relationship is balance. Knowing when to go full speed ahead and when to slow down and put it on cruise control is essential. As with anything else, too much of anything isn't good for you!

Over the course of years, life will give you an opportunity to learn. Learn from your mistakes, learn from others, and learn that there will be times when you go through things that have nothing to do with you, but more for the people who are watching you. Sure, the divorce was hard for you. The pain of no longer having him or her is tough, not to mention the looks of disappointment on your children's faces. But can you ever consider the people around you who are weak in many areas? They are looking at you and how you handle the situation. You could truly be the last push of motivation a person needs before doing something crazy! We truly are our brother's keeper!

Before you can become a great wife, husband, boyfriend, or girlfriend, you have to first be a better YOU. Switch things up a bit! Just because you've gotten this far, it doesn't mean there isn't time for an adjustment. Just as the world turns, so do people and their beliefs. Sure, stand on the solid foundation, but shift your thinking to better understand people and the world in which you live.

The reasons people are unfaithful can be for a number of reasons. I'm sure that if we truly looked at the seven deadly sins for what they are, we would find infidelity wrapped up in them in some form or fashion. Of course, none of those sins could force anyone to cheat, as we **ALL** have free will. But understanding why we behave in certain ways could give us insight as to why your mate decided to be unfaithful (even if you don't believe that God exists). You have to believe that there is something greater than you. You also have to believe that nothing good could come out of anyone doing wrong by another person. If we could see how we contribute to our mate's unhappiness, we might be able to alter the obvious course of destruction ahead.

Let's go a little **DEEEEP** here: How many times has your mate wanted to talk to you, and rather than listen with your ears and not your mouth, you use words like "It doesn't matter" or "I don't care" or "It's not a big deal." What if every time they tried communicating with you, you made them feel as though they couldn't be honest because you were always in your feelings? Or what about him or her feeling like they have to walk on eggshells in their own home? I'm sure if we spent more time doing an inventory on our own behaviors, actions, and words, we can probably think of a time when we shouldn't have said this or done that. No, your actions shouldn't make anyone cheat, but damn…it sure doesn't help!

The Roots of Infidelity Go DEEEEP

Deep-rooted issues are hard to deal with. Expressing those deep-rooted issues to the one you love is even harder if there isn't any support. Who cares that you don't desire to cook? If he or she is hungry, at least attempt to suggest something to eat or offer to get dinner! Just because you don't like watching Lifetime, set your Sports Center aside for a moment and watch Lifetime with her (there are actually pretty good movies now and then)! The point here is this: Don't expect your mate to change or bend if you're not willing to do the same. You may not care today, but at some point, when you start to care, those very words (or lack thereof) will come back to you ten times over. If sex is the issue (one that can definitely bring problems), fix it! As you are aware, a closed mouth never gets fed. Sure, everyone has their preferences in the bedroom, but one thing holds true: If you communicate about whatever the issue may be, it can be repaired. With the help of medical professionals, anything is possible. As a man, we may feel some type of way if we aren't pleasing our woman. Whether it be the size or stamina, if either is "off", it could play with our minds in a terrible way.

Be willing to make each other comfortable. Keep the lines of communication wide open. Find ways to make it work. Women, if your man knows he has your support while working through that 'sensitive' issue, it will make life a whole lot easier in the long run. Make your man feel secure. There are plenty of 'weak and insecure' men who will go on the hunt for someone else to please, all the while hoping you won't do the same. Know that outside sex is just that: SEX! Nowadays, what used to be sacred in the bedroom is on the table on day one! Oral sex is no longer taboo. You can meet someone, and the first time you have sex, one (if not both) of you are giving oral sex with no thought about who he or she was with earlier in the day or the week before. To make matters worse, you somehow convince yourself that it's okay if he or she is married or in a relationship, because somewhere in your twisted mind, you think they are only sleeping with their partner and you are the ONLY "random". All you can do is shake your head at the way some people allow their minds to accept what they are doing as right. An orgasm a day will NOT keep the doctor away.

The Roots of Infidelity Go DEEEEP

As you continue your quest for understanding relationships (intimate and familial), note that your significant other did not choose you to try and compete with your parental figures. Some of you are grown and still holding onto your parents' bosom like a child. If you want a man or woman to be like your father or mother, you should have married your parents! Being in a relationship means you understand that no other man could **ever** be your father, and no other woman could **ever** be your mother. Given this, you have to understand the growth process as well. People grow at different paces. For example, what I may have liked just last week may not be the same this week. It's called growth! Growth allows room for change.

If you don't take anything else away from this read, please take this: Life is not promised to any of us. Some will never see tomorrow — even though it's only a few hours away. Should you be the one not to see tomorrow, how would you be remembered? Do you feel that you have accomplished all that you could? Do you feel that at some point, you mentally matured in all of its fullness? If you have children, what will they say about you? Here's the point: Leave the past in the past. While it may be the reason for today's strength, it will not be the excuse you can exploit forever. Better yourself—**NOW**! You still have an opportunity in this moment to make the best of the rest of your life. Your past doesn't define you; who you will be does! Smile! Be happy! Be honest with yourself. Don't lie to yourself and expect others to believe what you don't. Leave the passive-aggressiveness behind. Be a better version of you! Deep down inside, you know your struggles better than anyone else. Dig ***DEEEEP***. Balance selfishness with consideration of others. Look at the person in the mirror and tell him or her, ***"You got this!"***—because you do!

I promise you: Once you become a better you, the mate you're **supposed** to be with is within reach. While you're waiting, be happy with and true to yourself!

ABOUT THE AUTHOR

Dewayne Williams

They say being raised in South Louisiana causes one to have a unique perspective on the intricacies of life—both good and bad. Born and raised in Lafayette, Louisiana, Dewayne Williams has that joie de vivre (exuberant enjoyment of life) that comes with just such a lineage. But that didn't come right away. He faced many trials before becoming the man he is today.

Through the various challenges life handed him, he has gained insight, determination, and a passion for life and being the best man he can be for his family, friends, and anyone whose path he may cross. He now desires to help those who find difficulty in helping themselves, and he is using his literary gifts to do just that.

Mr. Williams has been blessed with the ability to easily identify and relate to people from many walks of life. It is through these gifts that he can put pen to paper and bring life to his art in the form of stellar literary works.

Mr. Williams' most recent accomplishment comes in the form of a book entitled *Infidelity: The Roots of a Broken Man*. Today, he saw fit to expound on the topic with hopes of reaching individuals directly in that "uncomfortable" space with *The Roots of Infidelity Go DEEEEP*. Both books explore infidelity and its effect on families and individuals. Though some may find the books deal with taboo subject matter, infidelity is something that not only needs to be addressed and discussed; it is a topic that must be talked about to bring forth healing. The books seek to bring about dialogue concerning subjects that affect, in some way, shape, or form, the world's population in nearly its entirety.

Mr. Williams has a degree in Business and is currently working towards his Doctoral Degree with an emphasis on Leadership. He has plans to expand his brand globally, to impact as many as possible.

CONTACT THE AUTHOR

Author Dewayne Williams is available for guest appearances and speaking engagements. He can be reached via any of the following avenues:

EMAIL:

TheRootOfABrokenMan@gmail.com

FACEBOOK:

www.Facebook.com/Dewayne.Williams.9400

FACEBOOK FAN PAGE:

www.Facebook.com/TheRootsOfABrokenMan

INSTAGRAM:

www.Instagram.com/Dewayne_Williams05

Dewayne Williams

The Roots of Infidelity Go DEEEEP

LETTER TO MY FUTURE WIFE

To My Future Wife,

When the time comes for the two of us to live the rest of our lives together, I need you to know that I will do my absolute best to not only live by the principles of commitment but will also ensure that I be selfless when it comes to you. I want to give you the peace of mind knowing that while I will not be perfect every day, I will ensure I make a genuine effort to be perfect for you.

I know we will face challenges. I am sure there will be days when you feel like you want out. But if you will hold on to what got us to the altar, I promise I will make it better. I will lead us in a way that only a real man can; through living honestly, transparently, and dedicated – just like you do. Our children will see that what the world has to offer could never match what we have instilled in them.

I will love you unconditionally. I will not be naïve to think that our road will be peaches and cream all the way through, yet I will be equipped to take on whatever will come our way. Stimulating your mind, even if it's a corny way; I got that! Feeding you spiritually, even if you don't struggle in that area; got that, too! Craving you daily; yep, got that as well.

Dewayne Williams

Even if we face challenges in the bedroom, know that I will do whatever to fix it! Financially, I won't promise you a million dollars, but I can promise you I will work a million hours if I have to to ensure we are straight. If our families are different, that's cool. Let us be the glue that brings them together. If you or I gain weight, I will still love you. I will gain with you and lose with you. I will feed you when you're hungry, even when you're not thinking about food. Want to go out? Got that as well.

My point is that I will be the man who has risen above the sins that have so many trapped. I will be for you and you only! Infidelity will NOT be my issue within our relationship.

Until we cross that path, keep growing – and I will do the same!

                    Signed,

                    Your Future Husband

The Roots of Infidelity Go DEEEEP

FEEL FREE TO QUOTE ME!

1. Sometimes, you have to fall back silently and wait; your time will come. In the meantime, better yourself so you're ready when 'that' time comes.
2. You aren't getting any younger. Better yourself!
3. Never let a receipt or price tag define your worth. More importantly, don't let people nor pride dictate your decisions.
4. If you received $100.00 every time you've told a lie, would you be in a good financial place? So, then how much is being fake worth?
5. One of the best feelings in the world is knowing you won't stop until you wing big because when you do, everyone will win!
6. Old you, new you…still you. Do you know who that is?
7. Stop! Put this book down for just a second and go tell your significant other you love him or her.
8. Stop being on the fence. Pick a side and stay there. How much easier things would be if people knew where you stood!
9. The measure of a meaningful relationship is based upon the foundation on which it was built.
10. Don't be fooled! Envy surrounds you more thank you allow yourself to believe.
11. Transparency is a lifestyle. Don't try so hard to convince others about those things you can't see in yourself.
12. If you want to know who really has love for you, fall off, be broke, or say "No."

13. If you knew tomorrow wouldn't come, how would yesterday affect you? Stop letting the past control your future.
14. Strength is humility, and growth is transparency. Never allow what others see as 'weak' or 'fake' define you.
15. Sometimes, life throws you a ball you've never seen before or aren't prepared to hit. Just stay in the game and eventually…
16. Relationship goal: Learn what moves them. Then, move them!
17. Don't stay to prove others wrong. Stay because it's worth fighting for.
18. When you are with someone that you miss while lying next to them…ouch.
19. Do you hate that you love them, or do you hate that they see just how much?
20. The couple that's meant to be is the one who goes through everything that is meant to tear them apart, yet they come out even stronger than they were before.
21. The challenges you face today are simply the testimonies meant to be shared tomorrow.
22. When you think no one sees, that is when you are blinded by your own foolishness. Grow up.
23. When you know, you know!
24. All you can do is give 100% each and every day. Either they will see it or they won't. In any case, always be 100!
25. Affairs are way less about sex; they're more about desire—the desire for attention, feeling special, and important.
26. Like mathematics, relationships are universal in regards to its equation. $1+1=2$…not 3, 4, or 5.

The Roots of Infidelity Go DEEEEP

27. When you look in the mirror, do you see the same things people see when they look at you?
28. Don't allow irrelevant people or things to come between the two of you, for the two of you are better than those irrelevant people AND things.
29. Love yourself first.
30. Deep down, you know what it is. Stop stressing and losing sleep.
31. Certain things warrant a conversation; others, distance. Practice discernment.
32. So, they are good enough to sleep with, eat with, and hang with, but not good enough to be with?
33. You see them as weak. What you don't see is them trying to show you what real love and loyalty looks like.
34. Lying is a choice. Stop blaming them when you are the problem.
35. A closed mouth never gets fed. TELL them what you want and need. They are human; not mind-readers.
36. Not sure what's more disappointing; watching the cheating, knowing it's wrong OR watching them cheat and thinking you don't know.
37. Trust me when I say: People will wait until it's too late to see what God gave them. Keep leaving that old door wide open. You'll see…
38. Don't fall in love with their potential; fall in love with the real person.
39. Commitment = Are you dating someone? Yes! Is it serious? Yes! Versus today's relationships: Are you dating someone? I have a situation…

40. There is a huge difference between making a choice and making a mistake. You don't mistakenly cheat; you choose to.
41. The first step in changing is to become aware of your own foolishness.
42. It's amazing how drastically your life can change when you stop accepting the shit you hate.
43. Trust the one you're with or trust your gut! Trust what's being displayed right before your very eyes.
44. Does the truth really hurt? Or are you so used to telling a lie, the truth seems like a lie—and THAT'S why you get offended?
45. Deep down inside, you already know…
46. You can't be honest with yourself, yet you want someone to be honest with you.
47. If you display the same characteristics as a prostitute, why get offended when you're treated like one?
48. Wake up, already! They are showing you exactly what you're in denial about!
49. If you hang with ducks, does that make you a duck? No! But it sure makes you look like one. Are you hanging with whores?
50. Are you THAT lonely? You only speak via text…at times. When you see them, it involves sex (and maybe food). Holidays? Nope! Not happening. WAKE UP!

www.ingramcontent.com/pod-product-compliance
Lightning Source LLC
Chambersburg PA
CBHW071559080526
44588CB00010B/955